HUSTLE: PAY THE PRICE

Having **U**nlimited **S**uccess **T**hrough

Life-changing **E**xperiences

A Self-Help Memoir

by

Justin E. Maclin

Publishing: Maclin Motivation, LLC
Editors: Josephine Hammond, Everlina Hull, Sakiya Gallon,
Taylor LaCouture, Dwight Smith

Cover Photo: Joha Harrison
Cover Designer: Ashes & Roses Graphic Design Company

Instagram: @_maclinmotivation

ISBN: 978-0-359-09984-9

<u>What the People Think</u>

"Justin, this is brilliant! This is an excellent story filled with great examples of life lessons and so well presented."

Judith Moore
President of Tarik Black Foundation, INC.

"Justin it's so personal and sincere. You went through a lot. Somethings I never heard about. You succeeded in spite of all that confronted you. Your drug situation really touched my heart. Pain is a consummate teacher. Failure is always opportunity. Fall down once, get up twice. Your spirit is strong because you had a tremendous support network. HUSTLE is more than an acronym it's a lifestyle choice. Jesus essentially taught the same. I've always known that you would be successful at whatever you attempted. Those Oklahoma drills will teach you how to prepare for life. You may lose a few but never quit fighting. Never give up. Never doubt your God-given capability. Even when you lose, you somehow win. Because in a losing effort there is always recovery and recognition. You recover from the loss and you recognize what you must do next time to succeed. God bless you good Brother. You honor me by mentioning me in the book."

Apostle Bill Adkins
Pastor of Greater Imani of Memphis, Tennessee

Senior Editor: Sakiya Gallon-Johnson

When Justin told me he was writing a book my first reaction was "Of course he is". When I learned the title of the book my reaction was "How fitting." When he asked me to edit this book my external reaction was "Okay bet" but internally feelings of joy, honor and pride filled my spirit. I must say, that after reading this book I have gained a better understanding and new respect for who Justin is as a scholar, educator and friend.

I met Justin during my first year of graduate school at LSU and like others; I held some preconceived notions about him. He was tall, very slightly attractive, a former student athlete, and tatted—certainly not the "typical" graduate student. However, my biases quickly dissolved once I started to get to know him as a classmate and friend.

Justin was 1 of 3 Black men in our cohort of 20 students—and without a doubt the most hard working. If Justin called me on a Tuesday asking about an assignment, his first draft would be done by Thursday!

A natural born hustler—then and still— and the perfect person to write this book. Hustle Pay the Price is not a generic self-help book nor is it a simple memoir; it is a series of stories about personal battles, triumph, self-perseverance accompanied by words of wisdom and motivation It's Like Chicken Soup for the Hustla's Soul.

Foreword

Hustle: Pay the Price is an immaculate literary work of inspiration hinged on true wisdom. Applying knowledge is a lost art, and this stroll down memory lane infuses knowledge teaching life lessons with relatable circumstances of your peers. This book culminates the life lessons and wise ambition the older generations teach, but from the perspective of one who is the same age as its readers. I must say that this is one of the best written books-- storytelling ability, flow between story and topic, purposefulness-- I've ever read. It spoke to lessons I have learned but had not quite structured and brought about mind-altering ideologies that made me reevaluate my goals. Thank you for this work. It is to be appreciated and so are you. Being vulnerable in this way, and putting yourself on the line to be a voice of reason, hope, and perseverance to so many who need faith and guidance.

The chapter, Dying Young, took me away—the life lesson elaborated on in this portion is the story of our generation, I believe. I not only look at literal death, but our mutual friend you mention, as we both know, had a story that would have made for a movie and he was anointed. He did not survive to release the fullness of what he had inside, so not only did his life end too soon but so did his calling and blessing to others. In life, our minds are so fixated on materials and the allure of "success" that we have been indoctrinated with a false definition of what the word means and its purpose. We formulate our ambition around this misinterpretation of purpose not keeping in mind that our "dreams" are a seed and our abilities, character, and humility are but soil. Seed and soil do not create the harvest, but they partner with the external factors that edify them. God is the rain that is necessary to water the fertile ground and the sun that provides the light necessary for the harvest. Most amazingly, He is the external factor and created us, the seed and soil, in the first place. The way you frame this idea and expound upon its importance, prioritizing its place in our journey, is breathtaking.

I am proud to call you a brother from another mother, and honored to be a part of your journey. You, jokingly, say I am the reason you quit basketball, but little do you know I wholeheartedly say you are a major reason my abilities on the court escalated. You are only able to be as good as your opponent. If you play against mediocre talent then you will be mediocre. I had to begin my career playing against one of the best big men of our class. If I had, any hope of survival I had to match your greatness and aim to exceed it to come into my own. It was no easy task but since I embrace the obstacle, I became something no one could have fathomed, not even myself. You brought greatness out of me, just as Hustle: Pay the Price will challenge and provoke the same results out of its readers!

Tarik Black
Ridgeway High School Alumni (2006-2010)
University of Memphis Alumni (2010-2013)
Former Los Angeles Laker & Houston Rocket Basket Basketball Player (2014-2018)
Founder of the Tarik Black Foundation
Current Basketball Player for Maccabi Tel Aviv of the Israeli Premier League (2018-Present)

Table of Contents

A Birthday Message from Mom

November 6, 2018

Hi Justin:

     This is your mom calling to tell you "Happy Birthday." It was 27 years ago today that you were born, so of course I have to tell you the story of how I learned of my pregnancy. I was working at Walgreens when I started to feel very itchy. I figured I had hives due to some sort of allergic reaction, or that allergies were getting the best of me, so I made an appointment at Dr. Findley's office on Riverdale Road. When Dr. Findley entered the examining room, I began to explain my symptoms and concluded that it was allergies. His response was: "Okay, go back and tinkle in a cup." I went to tinkle in a cup, went back into the examining room, and waited for Dr. Findley to return with a diagnosis. A few minutes later Dr. Findley came back into the examining room laughing. Twenty-seven years later, I still remember his words; "You think you have allergies? No, you're pregnant." "WHAT?" I shouted, and immediately burst into tears; crying, crying, crying. "You're going to be ok," he said. "No," I explained, "you don't know my momma. She's going to kill me." Dr. Findley continued to reassure me and again stated; you will be fine." I left the doctor's office and went back to work. I called your daddy and said, "James, I'm pregnant!" He exclaimed, "What? You serious?" He was so excited and went about telling everyone in the University of Memphis' athletic dorms he was going to have a baby. In the meantime, I was dying of fear.

     Immediately after talking to your dad I called cousin Vickie, who was *working* at FedEx, had about 3 jobs and worked a ton of late-night shifts. I told her that I was pregnant. Her one-word reaction was, "What?" So that was that for me.

     What I remember most was Madea, my maternal grandmother and your great-grandmother, always telling me she was dreaming about fish. She would say, "Somebody is pregnant. You pregnant?" At that time, I did not know I was pregnant but I eventually found out I was. It was not until my fourth or fifth month that I told your granny I was pregnant when one day I walked into the house and told her I was going to move. "Why," she asked, "I hope you're not moving out because you're pregnant." My answer was, "I'm not moving out because I'm pregnant." She replied, "I hope you're not going to be shacking."

Of course, I was going to be staying with your dad; we were engaged, but we were not planning on marriage at that time. We moved into some small apartments in Perkins Wood. Your granny would call and harass me every day. "Lisa, if you're going to be over there shacking, you're either going to come home or get married." Though I was ok with being pregnant with you, I did not want to go home and be pregnant. So, I called your granny and told her we were getting married. I think she planned our wedding in 2 weeks. We were married!

I say all this to let you know you were loved and wanted. Once I told everybody I was pregnant they were excited and happy. Your granny spoiled me rotten and made sure that while I was pregnant, I was dressed well. I recall her telling me, "Just because you're pregnant doesn't mean you can't be cute."

You were a blessing to us 27 years ago and are still a blessing today. So, I felt that since you are writing a book that you could possibly add this to it, so people know that before you started "hustling and paying the price" you were loved. I love you and Pechone loves you. Happy Birthday!

Introduction

I have not always been the person that sat down to complete this book. I did not always possess the confidence that I now have, nor did I understand that I could successfully achieve my professional goals by sticking to my personal beliefs. In short, I was long on self-doubt and short on self-belief. What is self-belief? Self-belief is the ability to be confident in one's judgement and subsequent actions. It is recognizing why I exist at this particular place and time, knowing my purpose in life, understanding my life's mission, accepting the challenges that I know will come my way, and trusting and believing that I can positively impact others.

As a very young boy, I remember being extremely quiet and shy. I was a little chubby, had a small head—or so I thought—and awkward. My mother, Lisa Love, did not indulge self-pity. I recall her constantly reassuring me that I was special and would change the world. "Justin," she would say, "You will be a leader of men. You might be a preacher, superstar athlete, lawyer, or a model. I am not sure which one, but you will be someone who will change lives." I am not a preacher, superstar athlete, lawyer, or model but I did find a way to meet my mother in the middle. I am a former college student-athlete, a community advocate, and a motivational speaker to youth and young adults. And, thanks to my parents, I happen to be slightly handsome!

In my brief life, I have experienced events that have taught me invaluable lessons on how to handle adversity without being mired in self-pity. In other words, I learned how to overcome obstacles without getting "caught-up." I grew up in Memphis, Tennessee. A city with one of the highest poverty rates in the United States. I was blessed to have parents and extended family who were able to provide for me, but I had friends who were not as fortunate and at an early age became entrepreneurs to meet their basic needs. I remember classmates who sold candy, pencils, Pokémon cards and other trinkets to make money when they were in middle and high school. Then there were those who sold marijuana, alcohol, and prescription drugs. Obviously, one route was more acceptable than the other, but each involved a product, ambition, and a certain amount of risk.

My hustle started with my love of basketball and football. As a child, they were my recreational outlet, but when I entered high school, they became my hustle. I played both sports my freshman through junior year, but eventually concentrated and focused solely on football. Justin

Maclin was working to develop his talents into a product that would appeal to colleges and universities. Consequently, I had to make myself as valuable as possible by constantly working to improve my craft. Many mornings I would wake up at 5 a.m. to run with my father. I lifted weights and ran countless drills; often working so hard my body had nothing left to give. On two occasions, I was hospitalized for heat exhaustion and full body cramping. I do not recommend that anyone train to the point of hospitalization, but in the moment, I was determined to being the best football player possible. All of my hard work paid off. By my senior year of high school, I had achieved great levels of success. I was captain of the football team, received recognition as one of the top players in the state of Tennessee coming out of Ridgeway High School, and received a full athletics scholarship to Louisiana State University (LSU); my dream school..

This book aims to provide readers with my philosophy of HUSTLE; an acronym for **H**aving **U**nlimited **S**uccess **T**hrough **L**ife-changing **E**xperiences. According to Webster's Dictionary, *hustle* is "the ability to obtain by forceful action or persuasion, or to work towards a common goal." Missing from Webster's definition are the sacrifices, struggles, and/or disappointments that occur in the hustle process. Many times when I am "hustling," I encounter stumbling blocks or obstacles that tend to slow, but not deter my efforts. Throughout this book, I will share with the reader my personal journey, the obstacles and hurdles I have encountered in my life, but more importantly I will share how I overcame them. This is the philosophy of HUSTLE.

Drowning

In its 2014 *Global Report on Drowning*, the World Health Organization reported drowning as the second leading cause of unintentional injury death of children ages 1-14 years old in the United States— the majority of whom are males—and that most drownings occur in home swimming pools. Imagine a little boy who has never swam a day in his young life. He is standing at the edge of a pool, getting close, closer, and closer, and suddenly without hesitation, he jumps in! Not only does the child jump in, but he jumps into the deepest end of the pool; 13 feet to be exact. The water envelops his young body as he descends deeper into the water; he does not panic, nor does he attempt to swim. He is not aware of the grave danger in which he has placed himself. Before reaching the bottom of the pool, a hand grabs him by his shirt and pulls him up out of the water to safety.

The little boy was me, Justin Edward Maclin! It was a hot summer day and I was blessed with the opportunity to spend the weekend with my Aunt Ellen, Uncle Marvin, and my cousin, Marcus. This particular weekend, Marcus was invited to a friend's pool party and I was lucky to be able to tag along for the fun. I was 6 or 7 years old and ready to mingle with the big boys. I will never forget the excitement I felt when we reached our destination. When we arrived to the house, the four of us got out of the car and walked around the side of the house that led to the backyard. From a distance, I saw a beautiful, well-manicured backyard with huge trees and a pool with a diving board. As I started to run to the backyard, Aunt Ellen stopped me and said, "Justin don't get in that pool. J-u-s-t-i-n, don't get in that pool!" Well, of course I did not listen.

When she momentarily turned her back to talk to some of the other guests, I saw my opportunity to get in the pool. The kids swimming and playing in the pool looked as if they were having so much fun, and I wanted to be part of that experience. I walked to the very edge of the pool and stared at the water. I had never been in a pool before, but that did not stop me. I just went for it and jumped in the water! As I drifted downward, I marveled at the blueness of the water, the shadows of people swimming above me and the calmness of the water that provided me with a sense of tranquility. Because I did not know I was on the verge of drowning, I was not fearful. Fortunately for me, people outside the pool who observed me jump in and start sinking downward knew differently. One of Marcus' friends, realizing I could not swim, jumped into the pool and pulled me to safety. He not only saved me from serious injury or death, he saved me from myself. It is interesting how we sometimes engage in harmful activities knowing there are dire consequences; yet, we love every minute of the venture.

Once I was out of the pool and on solid ground, I had to come face-to-face with my frightened Aunt Ellen. After disobeying her orders to not get in the pool, I instinctively knew that this was not the time to have a face-to-face with her. I do not recall all her exact words but I do remember the directness in her voice, but it went something like this: "What did I tell you? Didn't I tell you not to get in the water? What the hell were you thinking?" She had never spoken to me in that tone of voice, but reflecting back on that day I know she was more fearful than angry about the situation which held life or death consequences. Needless to say, her anxiety and the reaction of the other guests filled me with a fear I had not before known. Consequently, it was a long time before I got into a swimming pool again. Fear held me back. My near fatal drowning on that hot summer day has profoundly shaped my life's philosophy. I wanted to swim, so I jumped in the pool without any regards to what could possibly happen to me. It just so happened I was saved by the ones who cared for me most.

You may be thinking "this is a great story" but I assure it gets better. Several years after my near drowning experience, my godmother, Katika Davis, taught me how to swim. Her three children were excellent swimmers and divers; routinely executing acrobatic flips and dives when plunging into their backyard pool. On one of my frequent visits to her home, she forced me from the edge of the pool into the water. She constantly spoke words of encouragement as she sought to calm my fears and anxieties while teaching me basic swimming techniques. I vividly recall her words, "Come on big daddy, you can do it. Just relax and everything will be okay." Not only did I learn to swim, I reached another milestone by learning how to dive—a major feat for a kid who had nearly drowned a few years earlier. That summer I faced my fear of drowning and instead focused on the rewards that learning to swim would provide. I had no idea how often Mrs. Davis' words would resonate and provide me with the assurance I needed when confronted by seemingly difficult situations, life-altering challenges, or the fear of taking risks.

Fear is a coping mechanism that helps to keep us safe. I have a fear of snakes, carnival rides, school mascots, and even clowns. Though I try to avoid encounters with them at all costs, if I do happen to encounter any of the things that cause me fear, my life will not be significantly changed. Those examples are unlike the fears that can be all consuming and can change life's trajectory. Starting a new career, moving to another state or country, buying a new car or home, or just walking up to that cute new girl or guy you see walking down the hallway, presents a risk that may provide negative or positive outcomes. I say take that chance, do what you believe in your hearts of hearts is right for you.

What does all this mean for me? I have learned that some rewards are worth the risks, and it usually happens that the more risk involved, the greater the returns. Living a life without the prospect of achieving greatness and happiness is for me similar to drowning. While taking risks instills in me a small amount of fear and anxiety, I also experience a high that comes with the anticipation of positive outcomes. If I do not succeed on my first, or even second or more attempts, I am okay with that. On my first jump in the pool, I did not learn how to swim! I needed rescuing and help was available. Throughout my short journey, I have had people who were willing to get into the pool to save me from drowning, and others who dedicated their time to teaching me how to swim.

My father, James Maclin, is one of my role models and a classic example of a man who works hard, dreams big and takes risks. Born and raised in the small, rural town of Covington, TN, located in the western part of the state, my dad graduated from the local high school where he was not only an outstanding student, but also a gifted football player. He received an athletic football scholarship to attend the University of Memphis, where he majored in mechanical engineering. At the University of Memphis is where my father met my mother. He and my mother became expecting parents and married during his senior year. A great college love story. After graduation, he accepted a position with a major real estate investment trust based in Memphis; successfully working his way up to a position as Senior Vice President.

In January, 2017, while I was attending graduate school at LSU in Baton Rouge, LA, my dad phoned with the news that his company was merging with another organization. He saw this as a chance to step away from the company he had worked with for many years and begin his own business. Naturally, as his son, I was concerned. This was the only place I had ever known him to work, and I thought he enjoyed the work he did. His reaction to the stepping away and deciding to go into business for himself caught me off guard; not at all what I expected.

This man acted as if he were the happiest person alive. My thoughts were, "Why would you leave such a great company? Why are you so happy? Aren't you at all nervous about taking this gamble on yourself?" He was excited because circumstances had placed him in a position where he was open to accepting the risks and challenges of fulfilling his dreams of having his own business. My pops jumped in the water and, with his wife Karol's, support; he headed for the deep end.

Each day he called to update me on his plans and the progress he was making in meeting his goal of becoming the largest African-American real estate developer in the city of Memphis. He sought mentorship from successful property owners and developers in the city, studied for his real estate exam, created a business plan, and mapped out areas of the city for potential development. Today my father has his real estate license, his own company, M&M Enterprise LLC, and has partnered with one of the oldest and largest property development companies in Memphis, Loeb Properties. Recently released a rendering and announcement of a $50 million development project located in the Art District of Memphis. It is safe to say that in spite of the risks and fears he may have had, he is now swimming in the deep end.

I hope you did not think I was going to go through this whole chapter without mentioning my mother, Lisa Love. Like most men who were primarily raised by their mother, I was always fond of her. I remember growing up and just watching and following her every move. If you saw her, you saw me. I have seen her go under water multiple times, but she always managed to make it back to the surface. I observed her strength and persistence as she studied for her bachelor's and master's degrees, all while working multiple jobs and taking tremendous care of me.

She often told me the story about when and how she discovered she was pregnant with me. Well, she actually tells me every year on November 6th—my birthday! According to my mother, having me was the best thing that could have happened to her, but I wonder if she felt that way when she initially realized she was pregnant with me and in the years after she and my father separated and divorced. I remember watching her crying out of frustration as she dealt with the realities of her life. It was difficult to watch but whenever I would see her frustrated and overwhelmed, I remember wanting to save her from her current situation. But, I could not. She relied on her own strength and that of her support system in the presence of my cousin, Vickie, and her childhood friends Nichelle and Michelle; all of whom were single moms with a son.

My mom is further evidence that sometimes when you are drowning, struggling, and/or experiencing turmoil, the best people to provide comfort are the ones who are just like you. "Teamwork makes the dream work" is a slogan we may hear casually used in conversation, but I saw first-hand how it made a difference in the lives of the four women mentioned above. The bond they forged and the support they provided each other was a beautiful thing to see. Now in their later years and with their sons grown and out the house, they are all successful in their own right. They taught each other how to swim, and through working together, they were able to navigate the deep end.

In my former position as Director of the Beach Athletic Club at Long Beach State University, my primary job responsibilities included community outreach and fundraising for the athletic department. After a brief tenure on the job, I had several big events under my belt and was receiving significant support from the Long Beach community. Drowning in my success!

I was feeling very confident as I worked on scheduling a small, intimate reception of 20 potential donors for a fundraising event at

Legends Bar & Grill in Long Beach, CA. I was surprised at how much smaller it would actually turn out to be. Twenty people RSVP'd, so I was expecting at least fifteen people to attend. Excluding me, my supervisor, and my intern, two people came. TWO! TWO PEOPLE SHOWED UP! I had ordered food and beverages for 20 invited guests with the intent of having a great time and raising a significant amount of money for the university, but only two of 20 invited guests attended. I was embarrassed, ashamed, and disappointed, as were the other university personnel. The event was a failure.

The next morning, I opened an e-mail from my supervisor, time-stamped at 2:38 a.m., so you can only imagine the way he was feeling; expressing his disappointment in the turnout and how we would be doing things differently from that day forward. I responded to his e-mail and was prepared to meet my doom when I went into the office later that morning. To my surprise, I was not reprimanded; instead, my supervisor, though still disappointed in the outcome, worked with me on strategies to improve outcomes for future events. He not only saved me from drowning; he was teaching me how to swim.

How powerful is that? He was willing to get in the water with me; swimming with me in the deep end of the pool. This same scenario has happened so many times in my life. I have been blessed with countless positive experiences; but I truly believe that stepping outside my comfort zone, and overcoming my fear of taking risks that did not necessarily assure positive, immediate outcomes has been rewarding. I have experienced first-hand how fear can be harnessed and become the motivator that drives individuals to pursue their dreams and reach heights they never thought imaginable.

Most of us have had experiences comparable to drowning, in that we may have experienced an event where we felt as if we were under water. But, one of the beautiful facts about life is that there are resources and opportunities for us to learn how to swim. Just get up and move! Even when you do not know exactly where you are going, as long as you keep moving forward, that is a start in the right direction. Learn to not be afraid to take the plunge, navigate through the waters, and swim to reach your goals.

Cutting Grass

Have you ever cut grass? For some it is a dreaded chore, something you do because it has to be done. For others it is a fun, relaxing activity. My mother falls in the latter category. When I was old enough to mow the lawn, I rarely had the opportunity to do so because she took on that responsibility. I vividly recall how excited she appeared as I watched her push the lawnmower back and forward across the yard. Cutting grass, trimming shrubbery, and planting flowers were her therapy and stress relievers. I did not relate to those feelings then and I cannot relate to those feelings now. On those rare occasions when I am asked if I have thoughts of buying a house, my first answer is always a resounding, "No!" While owning my own home is one of my long-term goals, I have no desire to take care of a yard. My childhood experience has convinced me that cutting grass is a skill that I cannot enthusiastically embrace.

As an 11-year old, it was tough trying to make money to buy the things children just had to have. I would beg my parents for whatever I thought I wanted at that moment in time, even when I knew they would say "No." I specifically remember asking for two things, Pokémon cards and a CD player. My father would say, "Justin, if you want those things go work for them. You need to learn that in life when you want things, I or your mother, won't always be there to give it to you." As I listened to him, I thought that there was no way possible for me to get a job. I was so young; I had never had a job of any kind, did not have work experience, and certainly did not have a marketable skill. I was in a dilemma with no viable solutions. I asked my dad what I could possibly do to earn enough money to purchase the items I wanted. He suggested that I cut grass and charge clients $10. Brilliant idea!

My dad's advice motivated me to device a simple plan to generate clients for my new business. I would use my youth and precociousness to persuade potential customers to provide me with the opportunity to mow their lawn. To my surprise it worked, in that customers listened to my rehearsed sales pitch. Now that I am older, I realize my ability to sign up clients had nothing to do with cuteness or innocence; the plan worked because I was addressing a need that people had. Successful businesses, from multi-national corporations to sole proprietorships, constantly market to consumers to determine their needs and/or wants.

As consumers, when we want a nice, comfortable pair of shoes, accessibility to the internet, or even a haircut; we are usually more than willing to pay for these goods and services, perhaps because we do not have the time or the expertise to make the items or provide the service ourselves.

I did not know it at the time, but I was advertising and marketing my services in an effort to make money to meet my needs; or in this case my wants. It sounded so simple. One of the unanticipated effects of my grass cutting venture was the excitement of the unknown. Before engaging one client or cutting one lawn, I felt as if I were rich, primarily because of the optimism generated by my belief that this business would be successful. The first step to becoming the person you want to be is to control your mindset and create an intrinsic system of belief in yourself. If you do not believe in self, why should others?

Sometimes success eludes us because we focus on the "want to," rather than the "get up and do." I wanted to be an entrepreneur and was willing to take risks to make my goals a reality. I like to refer to this idea as the "Come Up" method, or those times when your belief in self does not falter even though the odds are seemingly stacked against you. The "Come Up" method is simply when you feel you are at your lowest and make a strategic decision to take on a risk that could possibly change the outcome of your life for the better. When you are passionate about your beliefs and willing to let that passion fuel your work, you then have the ability to make positive changes in your life and in the lives of others.

Ready and excited to start calling on perspective clients, I made a mistake common to beginner entrepreneurs. I was so focused on the monetary side of the business that I failed to thoroughly plan for the operational side. I mentally asked myself these questions: Do I have a lawnmower? Do I have two lawnmowers? Do I have fuel to operate the lawnmower? How will I get gas and how will I get the lawnmower from house to house? It immediately dawned on me that one of the most difficult aspects of a business is the initial startup. This could have been a cause for panic; the objective was to cut grass, right? I went in my father's garage, which was full of random items and saw that we had two lawnmowers. One of the mowers was difficult for me to crank, and the second one was low on gas. What a way to begin my journey of becoming a working man --multiple dilemmas in a short period of time. As I grew older, I realized this was a part of life. The way we address obstacles and work to overcome challenges helps to shape our character.

We can give up and indulge in self-pity, or we can look for alternatives. I chose the latter.

The first thing I did was thoroughly search the garage for filled gas cans, but to no avail. I even contemplated how I could get gas out of the car, but that idea quickly faded. If I could possibly have gotten gas out of the car, it would have been a mini investment from my parents for my new start-up business. I searched for about five minutes before realizing that all of the gas containers were empty. Slightly disappointed, I resorted to the "ask" principle. "Daddy, will you take me to get some gas?" He said yes. "Daddy, will you help me start the other lawnmower?" He said yes. I quickly realized the power of just asking, which is something I now often do. There is absolutely nothing wrong with asking for help when you have exhausted all of your options; particularly when the objective is to serve someone other than yourself.

We got into the car and drove to the corner gas station and filled up gas cans. Returning home, we solved the problem I had with starting the second lawnmower. My father showed me what I was doing wrong in getting it to work. I was not pressing the pump start button hidden on the side of the machine. While he was showing me what to do and providing much needed assistance, I was brainstorming on ways to increase my grass cutting value. The answer was staring me right in the face the entire time. The key to making my business a success was to bring my father in as my partner. Intuitively, I knew I could accomplish more with his assistance. There is value in the strength of partnerships—provided there are shared goals—and it is a concept that I utilize in my personal and professional life.

Bob Beaudine in his book, *The Power of WHO*, writes of the importance of one's network using the 100/40 principle. He conceptualizes that individuals probably already know all the people they need to know in order to be successful. We often seek new networks of people outside of our family, friends, and close acquaintances. Fear prevents us from asking these people for help and guidance yet we are willing to ask a stranger to give us a job or give us advice. It is ironic that we will attend networking events, social outings, and conferences just to meet people we think will change our lives, when the people who sincerely want to help us change our lives and have our best interest at heart are right in front of us. Family and close friends are usually available and willing to help us reach our goals. Refuse to be blinded by pride and ask those closest to you for the help you need.

I asked my father to help me achieve my goal of making enough money to purchase a CD player and every Pokémon card in America. He readily agreed. There would be distinct advantages in partnering with my father. We could operate two lawnmowers and do double the work in half the time. But first things first; I had to get clients. My vision was to have the entire block of approximately 20 homes in my neighborhood as customers. Accompanied by my father, I canvassed the neighborhood, going door-to-door asking homeowners if we could mow their front and back lawns for either $10 or $15, depending on size. The number of rejections I received was surprising. Out of those twenty homes, only three households accepted our offer to begin mowing their lawn.

Rule number one in sales is being accustomed to hearing "NO," but I was having difficulty repeatedly hearing that word. Each negative response was money I would not receive. I made some quick calculations: 20 homes at $15 would net me $300, while 3 homes at $10 would only be $30. I would earn 10% of what I had the opportunity to make. I was not happy with those odds. I remember asking my dad what was wrong and why were people saying no. Their yards were hideous and badly needed the service I was providing. He replied, "That's life dude." The lesson he was teaching me was that in life you will not always get what you want, or what you think you deserve for that matter. He continued the conversation, "It won't just be handed to you. If you continue to push forward in this venture, they will eventually be calling you instead of you knocking on their door." That is HUSTLE!

I had a lawnmower, a partner, the ability and willingness to do good work, but I had not yet cut one yard. I asked everyone on our block to hire me; not missing a single home. From that setback, I learned that success requires hard work and happens over a period of time. I learned that sometimes you have to prove yourself by providing evidence that you can do what you claim you can do. I had to develop a portfolio of my work to show to perspective clients. I immediately put my skills to the test with my three committed clients. I mowed the lawns, pulled weeds, and edged those yards to perfection; all at a reduced rate. I literally put my heart and soul into cutting those lawns; allowing my work to speak for itself. Each lawn that received the Justin Maclin treatment looked like a smooth green carpet.

Just as my father predicted, neighbors saw my work and my lawn service began to grow. People took me seriously as a young man who wanted to work and earn money cutting grass. It was such an amazing feeling, but the most satisfying part of the experience was seeing the pride my dad had in what I was doing. I was paid my original asking price and most of my clients included a tip. Funny how that works! I expected to make $15 a yard, but instead I was getting $25 a yard. My business continued to grow as more neighbors, including some who had previously turned me down, sought out my service. I was filled with euphoria or as I called it at the time, "Making it." The feeling of "this is what I am meant to do"; of sadness replaced with joy; an overwhelming sense of accomplishment; the feeling of power. I possessed all those emotions. Needless to say, at 11-years old, I was rather cocky and arrogant as the adrenalin of success ran through my veins. I had to constantly fight to remain appreciative and humble—and I had parents who assisted in keeping me grounded.

Filled with excitement after being paid, I would go straight to Wal-Mart where I would purchase Pokémon cards, hot wheel cars, and whatever else I could with the money I had – a bonafide shopping spree. Filled with excitement at my purchasing power, I forgot about the CD player I originally wanted. In retrospect, I probably should have offered to give my partner—my dad—a share of my earnings. But I was a child, and I thought he had all the money in the world, and the reason I had to earn money was because he did not want to share with me. Flawed analysis, but I was a kid! As referrals increased and the business continued to grow, I was faced with new unexpected challenges: time management, lack of passion, and nagging questions regarding my "why."

Dctionary.com defines time as "the measure taken by a process or activity, or person doing it." As an 11-year old on summer break, I subconsciously started measuring my life in terms of time. The amount of time I had until the beginning of a new school year, the amount of time I had to actually have fun with friends, the time I had left before my lawn service would end. I was living my summer focused on losing time as opposed to fully utilizing my time. I still struggle with this in my adult day-to-day living. Occasionally, I find myself staring at my calendar and losing myself in time. My challenge is not to lose my time, but to use my time in meaningful and constructive ways as I pursue those things for which I am most passionate.

As the summer progressed and my lawn service business continued to prosper, I questioned my seemingly diminishing passion for cutting grass. Not only that, but there were concerns regarding the initial reason the business was started. I questioned my passion for Pokémon cards my desire to have a CD player - which I never purchased - I questioned my passion for money. All that may be good as in its not a big deal at that age or the stakes aren't as high for an 11-year old boy, but for most of us, as we mature, our passions change. However; the idea is to find that something in life that drives you and makes life fulfilling and exciting. My "why" for cutting grass was purely for monetary reasons; consequently, it was difficult to sustain my initial level of enthusiasm as each week I looked less and less forward to mowing lawns. What was once exciting and fun, was now a chore that I dreaded. I had to sit down and reevaluate what I was doing and why I was doing it. At first, it was the money, but later in the summer, I had an unexpected situation that would change this narrative.

It all started with my great Aunt Peaches, a high school teacher nearing retirement. One thing I remember was her constantly correcting my grammar, which she still does to this day. If I said, "Can I?" she would correct me with, "May I?" and if I said, "Ain't" she would quickly correct me by saying, "aren't." Aunt Peaches became a client I would never forget. She was the person who started me on my life's mission, the one who unknowingly helped me discover my why. It began on a hot Saturday afternoon in Memphis. It was summer time, meaning it was scorching hot! Through my father, Aunt Peaches reached out to me to mow her lawn and remove some dead branches. Her yard was one of those yards you had to take seriously because she wanted it to be perfect; mowed, weeded, edged, swept, and clippings bagged.

My father and I made a commitment to cut her yard, front and back. It took us a few hours to cut and edge it to meet what we thought were her expectations. It was a tiring, exhausting job for an 11-year old, but what I remember most was the experience I had with her after completing the work. My father and I went inside the house where we had water and some of Aunt Peaches' famous German Chocolate Cake. Man, that cake is one of the best in the country, along with my grandmother's peach cobbler, and my mother's pecan pie.

While we were eating, she went to her bedroom, came back moments later with a twenty-dollar bill, gave it to me and said, "Thank you." I looked into her eyes and took the money, but it was not the same feeling I experienced when I had cut other lawns, nor was it like any other payments I had received. I thought, "Why are you giving me this money? Why are you paying me for doing this?" I mowed her lawn without any thought of payment; I just wanted to do a favor for my Aunt Peaches. I enjoyed the fact that I could provide a service that she needed and one that would make her happy. This is when I realized my "why," or reason for living, and my passion. My life's why is to help others, my passion is to serve, and my life's goal is to be a servant leader. This is my hustle.

I clearly remember LSU Academic Center for Student-Athletes, Assistant Vice Chancellor/Executive Director, Kenneth Miles, who shared with students one of the best reasons I have heard for attending college. He would say, "We enter to learn, leave to serve!" This was a blueprint for life. While playing football at LSU, I had dreams of a successful collegiate career; perhaps followed by playing in the NFL. I loved playing for a football powerhouse, the camaraderie I shared with my teammates, being part of a group with a shared goal. We were a team and I played for them as much as I played for myself. My mother drove down for games and would tease me about buying her a nice house or fancy car once I graduated, but if that was what she wanted; I wanted it for her, not me. Football was not going to be my path to success; it was not my life's passion. Oftentimes, we accept jobs or start a business for monetary purposes. That is perfectly reasonable if your choices are limited, — and I am not knocking it— but you should be aware that it may not satisfy that passion that drives us to even greater outcomes.

I recall speaking to a group of young adults in the spring of 2018 when I was approached by a young lady. She asked a series of questions including why, in addition to my job, I wanted to become a motivational speaker, and if I were a paid speaker. She shared with me that she too wanted to work to motivate young people and wanted to know the fastest way to success. I asked her a few simple questions. How badly do you really think you want to pursue this avenue? Would you do the job even if you were not paid? Finally, is this something that you feel passionate about?

She replied, "I really want to pursue these ventures and I'm passionate about collegiate athletics, student-athletes, and I can be a great motivator, but I will not work for free." My reply to her was that she should really evaluate her why and honestly ask herself whether motivational speaking was a career for which she had a passion. Continuing the conversation, I shared with her that I completely understood the need for money, and that some of my past speaking engagements were unpaid, while many others were paid engagements. My ultimate compensation, is the happiness I receive when encouraging others and helping them realize they have what it takes to live out their dream. I left her with these words, "When you find something you would enjoy doing for free, you have found what you should be doing for a lifetime. Continue to search and remember to always be encouraged." The young lady is now an intern at Long Beach State University and volunteers in mentoring programs at multiple nonprofits in the Southern California area. When we last spoke, she had plans to establish a 501c3 organization to serve high school student-athletes by establishing programs focusing on improving educational and communication skills, and teaching financial literacy. Her story is a dream come true!

When I speak to youth groups, I occasionally receive inquiries about why I am spending time with them when I could be doing something else. I tell them that I am committed to a life of service and it is another opportunity to share my HUSTLE philosophy of life. This theory had its genesis with an 11-year old boy desiring to buy all the Pokémon cards in the world and a CD player to listen to his favorite music. It is the story of this same young boy and his first job, cutting grass to achieve his goals that far exceeded his expectations. As you continue to read his story, I challenge you to take a few minutes and ask yourself a few questions: Why do I do what I do? Who am I living for, not what am I living for? As you reflect on your answers, remember the young boy who started a lawn service for the sole purpose of buying stuff to satisfy his wants, but along his journey realized that waking up every day is another opportunity to serve others.

Balling Is Life

In a day and age when young men tend to play at least one sport, I think it is safe to say that for many, "Ball is life." The first time I ever heard the term was in 2012, while I was playing football at Louisiana State University. The football players frequently socialized with athletes on the track & field, women's and men's basketball, softball, and gymnastics teams. Of all the teams, the term was most frequently used by the men's basketball team members; particularly point guard, Anthony Hickey. He used the term religiously and watching him play, you understood that he meant every word every time he made the statement.

<u>Tee Ball</u>

When I hear "Ball is life," I reflect on my experiences and the amount of time I have spent on the baseball field, basketball court and football field. Sports made me happy and at other times made me sad; however, many of my most outstanding milestones are sports related. I recall my first true sports activity playing tee ball back when I was 5 or 6 years of age. For the uninitiated, tee ball involves hitting a baseball off a tee. It is "baby baseball" played by young children who have not yet developed the hand-eye coordination necessary for baseball. When not at bat, I played somewhere between outfield and first base where there was no action. Being around my teammates was fun, but the sport was slow and methodical and did not satisfy my competitive spirit. That first summer of tee ball was my last summer of tee ball. Since the hard work I put into practice did not yield the desired outcome or meet my competitive needs, I wanted to do something else. I think my mother felt the same way; plus, she just did not like baseball.

Taekwondo

This experience was the first time I realized the importance of competition and self-motivation in my life—even though at that young age I was not able to identify the trait. Working to improve my skill set in the pursuit of excellence has always been rewarding. Of course, I have experienced the stress of not meeting my expectations, but I wanted the rewards so I had to put in the work. I cannot begin to imagine how receiving rewards without the accompanying work would be satisfying. Skating through life without stress, worry, or concern, seems purposeless and may require reevaluation. The conditions I am describing are not ones that paralyze, but those that indicate a desire for excellence and being the best you can be based on your abilities. This is why I could not continue playing tee ball. I felt I was not making any meaningful contribution or impacting the game in a significant way.

I tried a number of other sports, but one of my favorites was Taekwondo. Hand-to-hand combat mesmerized me. Watching Jackie Chan in the movie Rush Hour with my father was one of the highlights of my life. The movie was funny with a bit of drama, but most amazing was Jackie Chan's, character Lee's ability to remain focused and keep his eye on the goal; the rescue of Soo Young, the daughter of Ambassador Han who was kidnapped by a Chinese Gang. Throughout the movie there were fight scenes showing Lee defeating as many as 10 men while running up walls, climbing fences, running through the streets, and/or severely injuring the enemy using his karate and martial arts skills.

I pursued this sport and loved it, eventually earning a brown belt. One of the challenges of moving from belt to belt was the test, which I often passed with ease, but became more difficult with each level. My passion for Taekwondo began to change when one day I attended a tournament/ceremony for the black belt performance. I instinctively knew that I lacked the confidence it would take to perform the ceremony to receive the black belt. The performance itself made me nervous and filled me with so much anxiety that whenever I recall that day, I relive those same feelings. That is one of my secrets my mother does not know; she just knew I started asking to do other things besides Taekwondo.

We often do this in life; find something we actually love but talk ourselves out of wanting to pursue it because of the fear of failure or humiliation. Fear of failure! We must not let fear control our lives. If you have something you want to do, make it happen. Along the way you may experience failure, but trust me, it is better than not trying. One of my regrets is not continuing to pursue Taekwondo, so much so that as an adult I have flirted with boxing and Muay Thai as extracurricular activities. When I say flirted, I do not just mean for conditioning purposes, but to improve my skills by sparring and immersing myself in the culture. Failure is the strength to try yet come short while regret is the outcome of weakness and fear. (Think about this. Not sure that is true. Look up the definition of failure and regret.) Attempt to succeed. React/respond to failure once it happens.

Bowling

After my embarrassing experience with Taekwondo, I shifted my focus to another sport. When I share this information with others, I usually have to call my mother to have her verify my story. Let us just say that I was quite the bowler back in the day. Not just one of those bowlers who went to the local bowling alley, rented shoes and used a random ball. No! I was on a competitive traveling team with my own personal shoes and a cool, colorful ball. To put it in perspective, one of my old teammates was Gary Faulkner, Jr., one of only two of the Professional Bowling Association (PBA) Tour's only African-American champions.

He probably does not remember me, but I remember him. Bowling became such a thing for me that even my mother began to bowl and develop a passion for the game. When I initially joined the bowling team at Winchester Bowling, I was not very impressive. Sidebars were put up to help acclimate me to the bowling lanes and to decrease the number of gutter balls I rolled. Everyone else was bowling normally while I had to put on the bowling training wheels. It was embarrassing, but I got past it and continuously worked on the art of bowling. I progressed from rolling gutter balls to finally keeping the ball on the lane, to hitting maybe three or four pins, to hitting seven or eight pins—until one day I finally found my sweet spot. This took a couple of months of hours and hours in the bowling alley, but I finally got it.

My confidence wavered from day-to-day, usually shaken by continuous low scoring games. Looking up at the scoreboard, my score was 55 points while that of my teammates would be 90+ points. Bowling taught me the power of perseverance and repetition. I worked tirelessly to improve my game and with encouragement from my bowling coach, parents, and teammates, I could not fail. I wanted to believe in me just as much as others believed in me. I became entrenched in the mindset of the the hustle; the time put into reaching a specific goal. I wanted to become a successful bowler, so bowling became like an addiction to the point that it influenced my mother to join a team. When you become addicted to success, others in your circle tend to share in that mindset of accomplishment. This is when leaders and leadership begin to take notice and become impactful. Success is in the routine and routine is in the foundation.

This is the approach I take. People often ask how I got where I am today? How did you start your company and why did you become a motivational speaker? My response is that I was passionate about it and became addicted to it. I constantly thought about my craft, practiced it, and sought ways to improve. Instead of calling me by my name, people would walk by and say, "Maclin Motivation," "Double M," or my favorite motto "Hustle: Pay The Price."

I credit my bowling experiences with gifting me this mindset. It was at Winchester Bowling Alley in Memphis TN that I learned how to create a competitive edge and confronting wavering confidence. Bowling taught me that successful people remain confident even when times are bad. Consequently, I went from the worst player on the team to successfully competing and actually showcasing what I had practiced. Unlike Taekwondo, where I was horrified to demonstrate what I had learned in front of others, I was actually looking forward to showing off my skills. There is something powerful about putting in the time and hard work it takes to get to a certain level and finally showcasing it.

Everyone on my bowling team knew how lacking in skill I was when I first started to bowl and everyone on my bowling team witnessed the progress I made over time. When it was time for competition play, I killed it. The game was not perfect, but my confidence allowed me to adjust my bad rolls into good rolls. Each week, my confidence which stemmed from my routine and set foundation continued to improve. And each week, our team continued to win.

After winning all of our local tournaments, the team traveled to Nashville, TN to compete. It was the first time I had traveled to another city to participate in any sport. This new experience was both exciting and nerve-wracking. Arriving at the bowling lanes, I saw the bowling teams but I also noticed something else; when I looked at the lanes, everyone was bowling at a high level. Most of the scores were at the 110-115 level, which was high for my age group. To make it even worse, besides my teammate Gary Faulkner, I was the only African-American in the bowling alley. Talk about an intimidating atmosphere.

Everyone in the bowling alley was cordial, but I still had this uneasy feeling which I've come to learn is a normal feeling for most black males in America; the feeling you have when you begin to doubt your skills and whether you have done enough to be at peak performance while managing the narrative that comes with your race. Challenging concepts to come to terms with at such a young age. My self-talk, which is defined as internal dialogue, was killing me. According to a statement made by motivational speaker, Les Brown, psychologists state that 86% of self-talk is negative. At this point in time, my negative self-talk was approaching 100%. I was feeling totally out of place, but that situation set the stage for future successes in my life. I kept hearing voices in my head telling me how I was not ready to compete at this level, how I still had areas to work on when it came to my bowling skills.

Often, we may experience periods of doubt and discomfort and at times we may tell ourselves we do not belong, especially as young black men. If you were to ask me if I ever feel that way now, perhaps I would say slightly; however, I quickly tell myself I do belong. I belong at the head of the table. I belong at the champion's podium. I do belong! Because of the way I have conditioned my mindset, I am often most comfortable in situations where others may think I would not be. I now thrive in these situations. Being successful requires learning to be comfortable in uncomfortable situations.

I mastered the ability to make myself comfortable in times of doubt by searching for that one thing that could make me belong. Even though I was intimidated in the bowling alley at a young age, I noticed that most of the bowlers felt that way. We wanted to win, we loved the game of bowling, and we were all human. Therefore, when confronted with difficult situations or the unfamiliar, I challenge you to find that one commonality and reason why you are in the given position and embrace it. When at work or other environments, living your daily life and you feel as if you are in an atmosphere where you do not know anyone, where you do not like a specific person or you think they do not like you, when you are in a situation where you fail to agree with someone, I challenge you to find this common space. Find your commonality. Find a connection.

In my former position as a development officer at Long Beach State University, one of my duties was to create meaningful relationships with friends and alumni of the university that would lead to financial donations to the university and athletic department. As a fundraiser, I was constantly out of my comfort zone. Remember, I am a young African-American male who was raised in Memphis, TN; a city with a population of 625,000, 68% of whom are African-American. This was in stark contrast to Long Beach State University where a significant amount of my time was spent at sports and community events, or at fundraisers with people who were at a minimum of twenty years my senior, of considerable wealth, and of another ethnicity.

They were all amazing people! With that said, it can be an uncomfortable situation for some. Many of my peers and friends asked, "Justin, how do you do it?" Even some of the donors said, "You're so young and different from what we are used to. Are you ok? Are you

enjoying it?" My answer was often, "Yes, I know they are different from

me. We have a mutual respect for each other and we have a good time

because we all want what's best for the university and its students, which

is our commonality and ultimate goal."

Reflecting back on the bowling tournament in Nashville, did we

win? No! Did I win? Yes, and no! I lost all of my bowling matches,

which was a horrible feeling considering I looked at myself as a true

competitor. But I won in so many other ways. I won because I learned

how to deal with adversity, to embrace my differences, to overcome my

doubts, and to persevere. I won because I became the hustle. I put

everything I had into reaching this one goal. I put my time, my effort,

and every piece of my mental fortitude into this game of bowling.

Basketball

Basketball is a game of skill and persistence; a game of rhythmic

movement and style. As I lacked all of the above. I first started playing

basketball at the local YMCA when I was 10 years old. Shaquille O'Neal

was my favorite player and I tried to emulate his style of play. I thought I

was a beast as I blocked shots and scrambled for rebounds. My godmother, Mrs. Davis, even called me Baby Shaq. Honestly, I was just

a tall, knock-kneed boy who hit puberty before my friends and lacking

the skill and coordination to block a shot. I recall my mother being

hesitant about even letting me play basketball at the AAU level. Most

people do not know this, but my old Uncle Marvin spearheaded this

campaign. On Sunday afternoons when my mother and I would visit, he

would ask her the same questions. "When are you going to let that boy

play basketball? When are you going to let him get on the court?" Her

response was always the same, "I'm thinking about it!"

Everything changed the day Uncle Marvin introduced her to

Clyde Peete, the man who would ultimately change my view of

basketball. Coach Peete coached the number one ranked AAU 12 and

Under team in the city of Memphis. The team was amazing, but I sucked.

I believed he let me on the team as a favor to my uncle and as a charity

case because everyone else on the team had skills. Some of the best

athletes in the country played for Coach Peete, including Clay Hilliard, a

short sharp shooter who was shooting from NBA range; Allen Farmer, a

feisty slashing guard who could play multiple positions; Masceo Howell,

easily the best defender I had ever seen at the guard position; Tim Peete,

a long, rangy player who could play all five positions on the court; Eric

Watson, a division one style athlete who also played point guard; and our star player Ronald "Tank" Brown, the number 1 player in the country at the time and probably the main reason I became a decent basketball player.

Our team was loaded with talent, and then there was me. I could not walk and chew gum at the same time. At the first few practices, I instantly shelled up and was intimidated by the intensity and speed of the game. I had never seen anything like this. It was rough! I was out of shape, missed lay-ups, and most of all I was SOFT! Remember that player Tank that I mentioned earlier? He was a 6'3", 12-year old—built like the Hulk—from Raleigh, Tennessee, who had a hard attitude and a chip on his shoulder. I would have to go against him EVERY SINGLE DAY! It was miserable. Elbows to the face, pushed to the ground, bloody days, and asking myself everyday if this is what I wanted to do.

Tank was the reason I hated the sport. Every day we played, he made me realize that if I did not step up to the challenge, he would remind me why I should not be there. This lasted for weeks. Whenever it was time to go to practice, I would get feelings of unease and self-doubt. Two people helped me through this turbulent time, Tim Peete and Big E--Eric Watson's father. Tim was my main man and still is today. He was the player who always made sure that I felt a part of the team,

considering the fact that I was shy, ashamed, out-matched, and the new

kid. Keep in mind, these guys had been playing together practically their

whole lives. Tim would invite me over to his home, text or call me.

Those seemingly small things were really big for me in a lot of ways. He

would say, "Just keep at it, you will get it one day. You are getting there,

just take it one day at a time."

I understand why he is now striving to be a premier basketball

coach; it's a natural fit for him. He's an amazing encourager and leader

of men. Tim was my source of encouragement. I refused to quit because

I actually had someone other than my family that believed in me. I do not

recall ever having that type of relationship with anyone, especially being

an only child with a few selected friends. Oftentimes, we do not fully

realize the progress we are making until the task has been completed.

Tim was the person who continually reminded me of my progress. I

would often mess up a drive and I probably looked like a complete idiot.

It was extremely aggravating and frustrating because I had worked so

hard; yet, I continued to not get the desired results. Adding insult to

injury, the rest of the team giving you, "That was bad. Do you think he's

going to make it?" look. Tim always gave me a look of confidence that signaled that I would make it. This same look transferred to Big E, a man who knew sports and wanted the best for his son and all the other boys on the team. He knew that if his son was to be a great player, the players around his son had to be pretty good as well.

He came up to me one day before the summer season and asked, "How good do you want to be? Why are you doing this? Right now, you aren't where you need to be to be a part of this team. If you decide today that you want to be something special, I am here to make sure you get there." My response was, "I want to be a good player and be on this team. Help." From that day forward my transition into a basketball player started becoming a reality. Every day for an entire summer, I met up with Big E at Airways Middle School. We did not just meet up there for a couple hours, we met and practiced for full days. Because of Big E, I became addicted to the game. We would do intense strength training and conditioning in the morning, basketball drills after lunch, and in the late afternoon our AAU team would practice. I lived in the gym and I gave my all to the game. BALL WAS LIFE! BALL IS LIFE!

The time I put in was paying off. My body was changing. I lost baby fat, my athleticism improved, and my basketball IQ began to click. I fondly remember an event that occurred during one of the team's practice sessions prior to the beginning of tournament play. This seemingly simple moment changed my mindset. We were doing our normal practice scrimmage when I had a first. One thing I had never done at practice was successfully box out Big Tank and get a rebound over him, but this time I did. Coach Peete immediately blew the whistle, stopped practice and congratulated me in front of everyone. Tank looked at me, shook my hand and also congratulated me. The work I had put in showed up and it paid off. I gave up my entire summer just for this moment; to be recognized and seen by teammates and coaches as somewhat of a success. I get chills thinking about that moment. I was a contributing member of the team and this is when my hate for the game became my love for the game. I continued this pursuit of basketball and riding this high throughout my time with the team. We won multiple tournaments nationally and finished twice as runner-up in the AAU National Championships.

Welcome to the game of football; a physical, painful, grinding, and Spartan type game. This is the game my parents wanted me to play. Slightly barbaric in nature, but nevertheless one of the best decisions they made for me. Initially not a football fan, I did not like the thought and feeling of being a sitting duck and being hit over and over again. My football career began when at the age of 8 or 9; my mom signed me up for our church football team at Cummings Street Baptist Church. We would practice during rain, sleet, or snow. Like, are you serious? I hated it. The coaches would make us do conditioning drills and "up-down burpees" in the mud with our football pads on.

Football is like the game of life; you get knocked down, get up, and make strategic movements to eventually end up with the desired outcome. The game brings together a group of men to accomplish one goal, and that is to defeat the opponent. If one man does something wrong, the entire team suffers. A successful football team is an example of teamwork at its best, even when there may be internal one-on-one conflicts that may test one's manhood. You can beat your individual opponent a million times, but the one time you fail to do what you are supposed to do against that opponent is the one moment everyone remembers. One of the best examples of this involves the offensive lineman in football, where the lineman can successfully keep the defensive lineman or linebackers from reaching the quarterback, but the one time they make a mistake and allow them to sack the quarterback; it shifts the momentum of the game immediately.

"Bull in the Ring." This drill is the worst. To let you know how bad this drill was, it is now illegal in all the 50 states. The players on the team would gather around in a big circle. The coach would have everyone call out a number and the number you selected was now your name for the drill. The coach would call a player out to the center of the circle and make the player chop his feet or run in place quickly; while doing that he would call a number. The player of the number called would then run towards the player in the center of the circle at full speed. The job of the player in the middle was to find him and brace for impact, which rarely ever happened as planned. 1, 2, 3, BOOM! The player would get up quickly for the next number. 1, 2, 3, BOOM! The player would again get up for the next number. 1, 2, 3, BOOM! The player is struggling trying to force himself up, but it is difficult.

This happened over and over and over again with different players. This drill could help build courage and toughness or it could fill you with anxiety and fear of the game. It caused me to want to flee from the game of football -- and Fast! I remember my first time performing the drill. I got hit once and did not get up. Embarrassed and feeling less of a man— I was eight and not a man— I got in the car with my mother and told her I did not want to go to practice again. She smiled and gave a slight laugh. In my mind I was thinking, "What's so funny? I almost died today." She said something very profound, "Justin, in life you're going to get hit and knocked down all the time. You can't just give up. You have to get up and try again. You will figure it out. So, you will be at practice tomorrow. Get ready."

We did the bull ring every day for the remainder of the football season. I remember hiding in the bathroom pretending my stomach was hurting just so I could either be late or miss practice. It never worked, but I learned that sometimes you just have to suck it up and tough it out. As I moved up to different age groups and different football teams, this same love-hate relationship for football continued.

I played for the S.E.M.A.A. Little League 49er's with the same hesitancy and dislike for football as the first team. If playing for this team taught me anything, it was how to lose gracefully. In my two years of playing for the 49er's, I think we may have won three games. It was demoralizing going into games with the idea that your team would lose most of the time. Even when we had the audacity to think we had a chance to win, we would get blown out. Now as an adult, I have more empathy for the parents than for the players because they have to watch their child continuously go through losing while maintaining their support.

During my time on the 49er's team I experienced both physical and mental challenges, which now looking back can be attributed to my transition into puberty. Mentally, I was weak and fragile. My mental weakness and fragility were related to being torn between not fully embracing the sport because it was not what I wanted, but rather because it is what I felt my parents wanted me to do. To understand my dilemma, it helps to understand that my father was an outstanding high school player in his hometown of Covington, Tennessee and a key player for the University of Memphis football team in the early 90's. He still holds a number of weight-lifting records at both of these schools. His teammates called him Big Mac and I was Little Mac. Like most children, I wanted to be like my father—and I still do—but after hearing amazing stories about his football skills, I did not know how I could possibly measure up to his talent. He was like a Herculean character and I felt like a big disappointment.

You may have guessed that I still was not an outstanding athlete, but my primary stumbling block was a lack of confidence. Playing for this team did not help. As with my previous little league team, we had a standard drill designed to build toughness and stamina that was performed every day. It was called the Oklahoma Drill, but unlike the bull in the ring drill where it was one person against everyone else; the Oklahoma drill was a one-on-one drill. One player would lie on his back with the ball and another player would lie on his back without a ball. The coach would blow a whistle and both players would have to get up off the ground as fast as possible. Once the players were off the ground, they would have to run full speed at each other and the player without the ball would have to tackle the player with the ball. The player with the ball could not run away, around, or make shifty moves. It was intense head-to-head combat.

When players would run into each other, it sounded like the roar of thunder. With the many concussion research studies completed today, we know that these types of drills were detrimental to players' health. Nevertheless, at that time they were common and considered safe. I routinely watched as players in line before me were repeatedly hit as hard as possible. I would sit and watch and pray that I would not have to endure this type of physical contact. I hid behind players and ducked away from the coaches hoping they would forget about me. Some days this worked, but most days it did not.

Curtis was the oldest and hardest hitting player on our team and we considered him the big kahuna. With ease, he would perfectly tackle and run over players. Curtis was the one person nobody wanted to have contact with, but for some reason I ended up going against him daily. He would run over me, over, over, over, over, and over again. It was as if the coaches were trying to force me to be tougher, but instead they were slowly and surely destroying my confidence. I was embarrassed. Imagine going to practice every day expecting to be embarrassed. It was emotionally taxing as a young child going to practice every day expecting not to be capable of measuring up to the other players.

No excuses though, child or not. I decided to be strong! I was determined to show character and made the decision that when I got knocked down, I would make every effort to get back on my feet. As much as I hated the hits, I was not going to be broken. I would put every ounce of my body and mind into changing the outcome and getting the results I wanted. Every day I put it all on the table, even risking potential injury. After a lot of hits, getting knocked down and getting back up, the day finally arrived when the tables turned in my favor.

Curtis and I lined up the same way we did every day in the Oklahoma drill. The coach blew the whistle just like he did every day.

And like every other day, I got up and ran at Curtis with everything I had in me. The only difference was on this day Curtis began to go backwards rather than running forward. In all the weeks of our going against each other, he never went backwards. But as he did, he hit the ground and fumbled the football. I had done it! I accomplished my one true goal of the season by successfully completing an Oklahoma drill.

My initial goal was not to win a football game or be the best player on the team with all the accompanying accolades. In fact, my goal had nothing at all to do with football, but rather I wanted to prove to myself that with persistent hard work and determination I could achieve success. Yes, Curtis was older, bigger, stronger, and overall the better athlete, but I was tired of losing. I was tired of failure and decided I had had enough; it was my time to be crowned champion.

Have you ever been in a similar situation? Have you ever been constantly beaten down to the point that you questioned your abilities? Have you ever decided you were going to stop those losses and defy the odds? It was a transformational experience when I ended the cycle of self-doubt and began to believe in me.

Yes, I lost some Oklahoma drills, but for the remainder of my time in this league, my losses were not as poorly executed as in previous practices. And, I never again had to go up against Curtis. My coaches taught me to never give up, but to continually strive until the desired outcomes were achieved. There will always be challenges and struggles that I will have to face. It is the way of life. I felt as if my beating Curtis led to a shift in our team dynamics that trickled over into the next game. We were at the end of the season and had not won a single game. Talk about a rough season on all fronts and now we were playing our final game. There was not a remote possibility the team would make it to the playoffs. In this last game and with nothing to lose, we were only playing for pride. Personally, I had nothing to lose, but I was running on high as a result of the best practice week I had ever had with the team.

The last game of the season, we walked onto the field around 8 a.m. on a misty Saturday morning that was perfect weather for football. It was customary for teams with losing records to always play the early games. The team coach came onto the field and gave us words of encouragement despite our losing season. He spoke of the amount of growth he saw in us through the season, how proud he was of us, and how we left it all on the field every game. Surprisingly, he also thanked us. Team members looked around at each other in confusion trying to figure out why he would thank us for a winless season. As he continued speaking, he explained that though we never won a game, we inspired him to keep pushing, to keeping striving, to keep going because he was experiencing some difficult personal problems. "Seeing you battle with a sense of pride every day during times of defeat, I couldn't give up because things weren't going perfectly for me. You all are the true champions. You all saved my life."

Can you imagine the impact hearing those words of inspiration had on the team moments before we were to take to the field? Wow! You never know who you might be encouraging or unknowingly helping just by showing up and putting forth your best effort. Coach's speech gave us a new purpose and new motivation. We wanted to end this season with a bang for coach. He deserved it, I deserved it, we all deserved it. The team captains went to the center of the field for the coin toss. Unlike previous games we played, this morning just felt right; as if we had a chance of winning. Our team won the coin toss and deferred. This meant we would put the pressure on our defense first and we would get the ball first after half-time. On the first play, our opponent broke for a big run; second play, our opponent broke for a big run; third play, they broke for a big run, but the running back dropped the football! We received the ball and scored.

The game would continue this way to the end. It was as if every time the other team would get some steam and momentum, our team would cause something to happen that was in our favor. During the game, I felt unstoppable with a new-found sense of relevancy on the team. Now, I felt like the Big Kahuna. It is amazing how reaching just one of your goals can have such a positive impact and generate enormous confidence. We beat the other team by a score of 21-7. This was the first time all season our team scored more than one touchdown. We won! Most of all we proved to ourselves we could actually do it. All the days of doubt, lack of trust, insecurity, and confusion evolved into a bond of brotherhood, family, love, and belief. We celebrated as if we won the championship game.

We were not awarded a championship trophy; rather, we received an intangible trophy celebrating winning at life. Coach was so proud of his team that he broke down and started to cry. It was a scene out of the movies. We had done it. The season was over, but I wanted to continue playing. The team I dreaded at the beginning of the season was now the team that brought me so much joy. That was a season of constant transition and a season of personal growth. The successful achievement of one goal was like a chain reaction, generating more and more positive outcomes. Ball is life!

Shining Stars

First thing first, God's guidance in my life and the role he plays in putting me and all of us in situations for our good causes us all to be shining stars because we are made in the image of Him. Growing up, I spent a majority of my life in the Memphis area known as Hickory Hill; primarily a working-class African-American and Hispanic community that was in transition. We lived comfortably and had great neighbors like our next-door neighbor, Miss Margaret, who cared for her extended family and also looked after me when my mother needed her assistance. Directly across the street from our home was one of the largest houses in the neighborhood that was occupied by a large Hispanic family. Our other next-door neighbor was a single mother trying to make out a living. On occasions, I awoke early in the morning to assist her in delivering the daily newspaper. Those were long mornings.

To my mother's credit, the home that stood out most in the neighborhood was the one owned by Lisa Love. She constantly made upgrades to the home, one of the smallest houses in the neighborhood. We were living in the Landings Apartment in East Memphis when she decided to purchase a home for us. She looked at the house and, as I recall, it was on the market for roughly $83,000. When I saw that price, I thought she was one of the richest ladies alive. The outside of the house was a hideous brown color and inside practically everything was pink, the floors were pink, the walls were pink; everything was pink. It was scary, especially for a young boy.

To my surprise, she purchased the house. During this period, my mother was a teacher at Ross Elementary School, the neighborhood elementary school. After moving in, she installed new carpet and made additional interior upgrades. She changed everything about the home including painting the brown exterior to a sky-blue color with a white trim. It was a cute house that stood out among all the houses on the block. While she continually made upgrades, other homes in the area were continually deteriorating as the number of homeowners decreased and the number of renters in the neighborhood increased. More and more homes were abandoned.

Though the neighborhood was declining, my mother still took pride in our home and continued to make improvements inside and outside. My mother refused not to shine. People frequently ask me who I admire most in this world and I always give what may appear to be a cliche response. My mom! Anyone who knows me well, knows that I love that lady. While rearing me, I witnessed the stress she endured as a single, working mother. Many of us know, or have heard stories of, strong, nurturing, African-American single mothers. My mother worked long hours at her job (still does), drove me all over the city to different practices, prepared our meals, and nurtured her students, especially those from dysfunctional families. She experienced multiple deaths of close family members in a short period of time. I watched the toll that the stress of these experiences took on her, but I also saw her face challenges head on and overcome her adversities. She made positive things happen as she decided that regardless of her circumstances, she was going to shine.

But what is shining and what does it mean to truly shine? How do we make this possible? As a child I would often sit on the back porch alone at night. No one ever knew about these solitary moments that were so peaceful and reflective. The back porch was my first private little sanctuary. When I would do something, I was not supposed to, or during times of distress, I would sit on the small porch and commune with nature. So many questions were answered on this porch; some simple, others more complex and thought provoking. What should I wear to school the next day? What is my purpose in life? Am I the person I am meant to be? Why don't I understand what's going on with me and why do I feel so empty? Often as I gazed into the clear, dark sky of sparkles, I would often hear Lil Wayne's, *Sky is the Limit*, playing in my head.

Prior to relocating to Davis, CA, I lived in the beautiful and scenic beach city of Long Beach, CA, where the pier became my new place of sanctuary. I often was frequently in deep thought as I would watch the stars twinkling one, two, and three at a time. They shined so brightly and I was captivated by their beauty and rhythmic display. Sometimes when I thought of stars, they were not the literal stars in the sky, but people who were successfully living rewarding, purposeful lives. At this time, I put the two together and I asked myself a series of questions that needed answers. "Do I deserve to shine and shine as brightly the stars in the sky? Do I deserve to shine like the many people I admire? Do I deserve this? Do I know what it means to shine? How can I shine?"

When I conduct speaking engagements at high schools, colleges and universities, or other venues, I ask the audience these same questions. The looks on their faces say it all. We are wired to question our abilities. Can I do this? Should I do this? What would doing this do for me? Why don't I deserve this? Why can't I do this? What will keep me from accomplishing my goals? The list of questions is endless. It is as if we have to go through a defeatist process before we accept the idea that we have endless possibilities and opportunities to live the life we want for ourselves. When I say this, I am reminded of the math equation that two negatives equal a positive. So, let us break these questions down.

Pause for a second and ask yourself, do I deserve to shine? The easy answer is yes, everyone does. We were created for great things and we all deserve opportunities to be our best selves. If we are honest with ourselves, most of us delight in the recognition we receive when we act unselfishly. I believe we are wired to run off fuel given to us when we are making positive impacts in our world.

Have you ever just done something as simple and kind as to give a homeless man a dollar? Did you see the smile on his face? Do you remember the warm feeling you received from doing so? Did you notice how his gratitude caused you to glow? At that moment, you were shining! You made an impact. You not only made an impact, but you made a conscious decision to make an impact.

We frequently question whether we deserve to shine when we are at our lowest point and or indulging in self-pity. It could be failure to pass a test needed to graduate or failure to get the raise you so richly desired. It could be job loss or the end of a long-term relationship. There are a myriad of reasons and situations that cause us to question why we do not reach our full capabilities.

Recently, I reconnected with an individual with whom I had a past relationship. We did not talk for a full year; a full year of no communication. That is until one morning when I woke up at my normal time of 5 A.M, looked at my phone and noticed that I had a text message from her. I was shocked. It took me a while to text back but I did. She shared with me the turmoil she had experienced during the previous year.

In one year, she had developed a slight alcohol addiction along with an eating and sleep disorder. Her behavior caused friction between her and members of her family. In addition, she was involved in a traumatic automobile accident. As I listened to her describe the pain she had endured, I instantly became worried, but then she made a statement that caught me totally off guard. "Justin, I went through a lot this year. Wished you were there, but you not being here helped me. I faced all these different situations I could have never imagined for myself, but one day I woke and I said, no more. I deserve better and I will be better." She told me how she took all that pain and made it her reason to be better. She changed her entire lifestyle, lost 20 plus pounds, and graduated with her MBA in a year. She moved out of her parents' home and became more independent. More importantly she made the decision to forgive me; not only forgive me, but reach out and talk to me. She is a strong woman who became assertive and took control of her life. She decided that she deserved to shine, and in my eyes, she will forever be a star.

Still don't believe you deserve to shine? My experience in graduate school is a prime example of shining. I attended graduate school at Louisiana State University, where I received the Masters of Higher Education degree. Graduate school was one of the most intimidating experiences of my life. To be successful, I was forced to become a true academician, which was never one of my strong suits. We are talking about a kid who barely got into college, made a 17 on the ACT, struggled academically in college and could have easily ruined his opportunity to earn an undergraduate degree.

I had never seriously thought of graduate school until I was approached by one of my college mentors, Verge Ausberry, shortly after receiving my undergraduate degree. He said to me, "Justin, go to graduate school!" I researched what I needed to do. Graduate school applicants had to complete an application for admission, take the Graduate Record Examination (GRE) and pass with a certain score, and pay the tuition. I was immediately faced with three concerns: 1) I did not know the program of study I wanted to pursue; 2) I had no idea how to prepare to study for the GRE exam; and 3) I was broke and did not know how to pay for the program.

I became an investigator and sought information from some of the successful people on campus who held positions in which I was interested; reviewing both their undergraduate and graduate degrees. When possible, I asked for a meeting to receive input that would assist me in making an intelligent decision. The consensus was that my chosen career would be enhanced by a graduate degree in Higher Education. That was the easy part, but it quickly became more difficult. The next course of action was to make preparations to successfully complete the GRE with a score high enough for acceptance into the graduate program.

Taking the GRE would be the most difficult part of the process. I am not a good test taker and the GRE was a three-hour exam, which required a minimum score of 150 for admission to graduate school. I studied day and night for 2 months with my friend, Joe Hollins, who provided tutoring and testing tips. The day finally arrived for me to take the GRE. To my amazement I completed the test in 2 1/2 hours. I worried whether that was good or something worse. Fortunately, score results are available almost immediately after completing the test; thus, eliminating the stress of a long wait before knowing the outcome. My prayers were answered when I learned my score was 152. I experienced a tremendous amount of relief when it sunk in that I could do this post graduate thing. Though mentally ready and prepared for the challenge, I lacked adequate finances.

During my undergraduate years, I was a student-athlete on full scholarship; therefore, I did not have to worry about paying tuition. If I were to attend graduate school, I would be responsible for paying tuition. Consequently, I applied for multiple graduate assistantships in athletics, such as marketing, academics advising, and event management. If a scholarship was available, I applied for it. Graduate assistantships paid tuition and provided a small stipend for living expenses. Sounded like a good deal to me. I submitted an application and received the graduate assistantship in the LSU Cox Communications Academic Center for Student-Athletes; working in the Shaquille O'Neal Life Skills Department. This was additional proof that I deserved to shine!

In the span of a month, I was accepted into graduate school complete with funding to sustain me for the years it would take for completion. Life was good, but as is usually the case, without warning I ran into my first road block. The graduate assistantship only paid for tuition; not university fees. I woke up early one morning with a plethora of emails stating that I owed the university money. I panicked and immediately sought out my supervisor for an explanation. He explained that university fees were due prior to starting school and without payment, I would not be able to attend classes. I immediately called individuals I knew seeking a loan. All my replies were negative. Distraught and without any immediate viable options, I burst into tears in my supervisor's office. I was embarrassed, but as I sat in his office, I knew what had to be done. With his assistance, I completed the paper work for a student loan. I was now officially a graduate student.

Let me paint you a picture. It is August of 2015, day one of graduate school. I woke up excited about the day and my new venture. As I anticipated the beginning of another level of success, I was both anxious and excited. I walked into my first class and immediately became aware of stares from the students and professor. It was the all too familiar, "Why is he here?" look. He is an African-American male and former student-athlete walking into a graduate classroom where he does not belong. I was highly offended by the unspoken assumption that as a student-athlete I was given grades and had not legitimately earned the right to be in the class. I had worked hard to earn my spot in that classroom and I would not be dissuaded.

My first reaction was hurt, followed by anger. I decided day one of class that I was going to shine. To show that I meant business, every day I came to class dressed in a button up shirt and tie. I was on a mission and to prove my point, I would work harder than anyone else in that class and become the star of my cohort. When I had a paper due, it was submitted weeks in advance of the due date. I learned that with early submission I could get feedback from my professors or other classmates in time to correct errors and resubmit. My productivity and work ethic earned me the respect of my professors and classmates; some of them describing me as 'a man possessed'. No one in that class was going to out grind me.

During a particular lecture session, Dr. Jennifer Curry, in whose class I was enrolled, posed a question to the class, "Who wants to get their doctorate?" Though not absolutely certain that this was what I wanted, I nevertheless was the first person to raise my hand; at least demonstrating a willingness to explore the possibility. Dr. Curry, aware that I had previously expressed interest in pursuing a doctorale degree, offered me an opportunity to work with her on a study which was later published in several academic journals. The qualitative study, *African American Student-Athletes Perception of Their College Preparedness,* took a year to complete. Using the LSU football team as subjects, the study sought to identify disparities in academic achievement between African-American students who attended K-12 educational systems in the inner-city and white students who mostly attended suburban schools. Dr. Curry and I presented the paper at several conferences in Louisiana.

Before attending my first class, I made a conscious decision that I would not just do enough to get by, but I was going to set a standard for other student-athletes who entered this program or had aspirations to attend graduate school. My motto: When you combine hustle with a positive mindset, you will shine.

Becoming Legendary

One day walking across the campus of Long Beach State, I was engaged in a conversation with the individual whose job included marketing and imagery for the university. For over three years, he had been working on a rebranding project; putting forth proposals with varying degrees of acceptance.

His final and most contentious project was assisting in identifying a replacement for the university's controversial mascot, Prospector Peete, who was considered a negative connotation of indigenous people. Some suggestions for a new mascot included a shark, stingray, wave, and other animate and inanimate objects. Though not official, some on campus half-heartedly referred to themselves as *The Beach*.

I asked my friend to share his thoughts on replacing the mascot. "I have a few in mind," he stated, "but the one that immediately comes to mind is *Legends*. Long Beach State Legends." I asked why? His answer gave me something to think about. "What are our students' main goals when they come here? What are our goals as employees? What do our athletes strive to be on the playing field? Legends!" He continued his explanation as he described how students and employees worked to make positive and unforgettable contributions to the university. His sense was that individuals wanted to participate in and be part of a program that was legendary. His explanation caught me off guard.

The name Legends was meant to express an ideal, as opposed to an object or thing. I was intrigued by the conversation as I begun to reflect on how individuals are identified and what it means to be legendary. Did I know any legends, and if so, who were they, and why were they considered legendary? I asked all of these questions, and when I ask questions, I look for answers. I went into research mode to differentiate between legend and legendary. I thought they would have two totally different meanings; however, the definitions were similar.

According to dictionary.com, a legend is "a collection of stories about an admirable person," while legendary is defined as "of, relating to, or of the nature of a legend." When I think of legends, yes, I think of people who are famous and/or well known for their abilities or contributions to society. Some people who readily come to mind are former President Barack Obama, Nelson Mandela, Oprah Winfrey, Bill Gates, Muhammad Ali, Mahatma Gandhi, and Jeff Bezos to name a few.

These people used their talents to make significant, positive changes for a large number of people.

I am reminded of Dr. Martin Luther King, Jr., whose life was dedicated to fighting inequality in a non-violent manner and I frequently reflect on his still timely *I Have a Dream* speech, delivered at the March on Washington in 1963. A legendary speech delivered by a legend, who earned the 1964 Nobel Peace Prize.

However, I also think of individuals who make or have made a major impact on others' lives while not being as famous or widely known. They are legends because they impacted the lives of those with whom they had contact; influencing them in ways that will not soon be forgotten. One such man was Arthur Moses Hull, my grandfather and mentor. I called him granddaddy. Granddaddy was a well-known educator in the then Memphis City Schools system. I especially remember his tenure as principal of A. B. Hill Elementary School where I spent many afternoons with him. My mother, who had aspirations of becoming a principal, was mentored by granddaddy, and I was nearly always with her when she went to the school. My granddaddy was a good man and was loved by many. My grandmother often said that something was wrong with the person who did not like Arthur Hull. That was not an exaggeration! We spent an enormous amount of time together; going to movies or buying ice cream, and doing all the amazing things kids love to do. He was my hero and I admiringly looked up to him in every way.

In 2009, granddaddy developed pneumonia and was hospitalized. Ensuing complications caused him to be hospitalized for weeks, followed by what was to be a brief stay in a skilled nursing facility for a full recovery. One afternoon when I visited him, he shared that he would be released the following day and that we were going to be able to go to the movies like old times. Following was a night I will never forget. It was a school night and I was asleep in bed when my mother came into my room.

"Justin," she said. "Wake up. I have to tell you something. Arthur passed away." This was one of the most difficult times in my life because I seldom thought of people leaving this world; especially people like my grandfather. What made it even more painful was that we had made plans to spend time together the following day when he was released from the nursing facility.

Several days after his passing, funeral services were held. I was astounded by the many people in attendance. I saw an endless stream of people I did not know entering the sanctuary of Mt. Pisgah C. M. E. Church, his family church in the Orange Mound community where he was born and reared. Approximately 500 people, excluding family members, were in attendance because of the impact my grandfather had on their lives. The range of mourners was diverse; childhood friends, educators he had mentored during his career, students he had taught in his 30 years in the school system.

For days and weeks following my granddaddy's funeral, family and friends consistently reached out to the immediate family in honor of my granddaddy. I was amazed by the stories I heard of my granddaddy's generosity and the things he had done for others. I knew there was a reason I admired and loved Arthur Hull and wanted to be like him. He is indeed a legend.

Whenever I return home to Memphis, I am reminded of him in many different ways. My grandmother's and close family members' method of acknowledgment when I have done something positive are these words, "You remind me so much of your granddaddy, he would be so proud of you." On several occasions while walking around a mall or at a popular restaurant, people have approached me and asked, "Are you Arthur Hull's Grandson? He was amazing and taught me everything I know. He is the reason I am successful now and have a great family." He is not forgotten. He is remembered for the good he did and the respect he had for individuals regardless of their circumstances. He left a lasting legacy and made a significant impact on those with whom he had contact. He is legendary.

How do we become people with the same type of character Arthur Hull possessed? How do we become legends in a cynical society that primarily focuses on the famous and sometimes infamous members of our society? On a personal note, I ponder how as an individual I can make a positive impact and what will be my legacy. I believe I have my answer when I strive to lead people to follow their dreams and live a purposeful life. People can feel when you are passionate about something and living in your purpose. In that passion, you inherently give off positive vibes that lead to belief and hope for everyone.

I first realized this when I worked in the Life Skills Department for Student-Athletes at LSU. It was my job to promote community relations by building outside partnerships with Baton Rouge non-profits and engaging student-athletes in community service projects within those organizations. This position also afforded me the opportunity to mentor students in K-12 schools and multiple other programs. I was able to assist students in many different areas of need; find jobs, earn internships, meet graduation requirements, apply for college, and more. These activities were the foundation to discovering, not only my life's purpose, but gave me the confidence to become a motivator, a writer, a mentor, a coach, an entrepreneur, and a public speaker.

The first time I spoke publicly was at the prompting of my Life-Skills supervisor. He entered into the office where I was working and casually said, "Justin, you've had some obstacles during your stint at LSU as a student-athlete. You've been through some tough times growing up in Memphis and I need you to talk about it." Then he added, "tonight." I humbly agreed, though not quite sure exactly what he wanted me to do.

I walked into the LSU Cox Academic Center for Student-Athletes auditorium and seated before me were over 100 freshman and sophomore students. I was tasked with motivating them to take college seriously and not take being at this specific institution of higher learning for granted. I started speaking and the feeling was both chilling and exhilarating. Though at first nervous, once I connected with the students, I knew this was my life's purpose. At the end of my speech, the positive feedback I received communicated the idea that I had made a positive impact on those present.

A surreal feeling came over me because I was speaking about something for which I had a passion. It is the feeling when you become one with yourself and your audience. I think of it as being comparable to a basketball player who is on a scoring rampage and has not missed his last 15 shots and scores over 40 points in a game. When asked about his performance, he may respond with a statement similar to, "I was in the zone, the basket just seemed to get bigger and bigger after every shot I made. The crowd seemed to get louder and more engaged after every shot I made and the gymnasium lights seemed to get brighter and brighter. It was as though a higher power was telling me this is what I am meant to be doing."

This is the feeling I have when I am speaking to groups; it just feels right. When I connect with the audience and feel the shift in the room, chills go through my body. With each word, I feel the countless hours of practicing and studying is paying dividends. Every day I wake up and wonder how I can become more like my granddaddy, a man whose 30-year tenure as an educator is still making an impact; a man who cherished family and friends alike.

James Allen, writing in his book, *From Poverty to Power*, asserts that, "Happiness is that inward state of perfect satisfaction which is joy and peace, and from which all desire is eliminated. Self is blind, without judgement not possessed of true knowledge, and always leads to suffering. Cling to self, and you cling to sorrow, relinquished self, and you enter into peace. To seek selfishly is not only to lose happiness. As we realize that all-embracing love which is negation of self, we put ourselves in harmony with divine music, the universal song, and that ineffable melody which is true happiness becomes our own. You need trust, generosity, and love to realize true prosperity. The heart that is not possessed of these qualities cannot know prosperity, for prosperity, like happiness, is not an outward possession, but an inward realization."

When I reflect on the meaning of legendary, I reflect on this passage. We can all strive to be legends in the sense that we positively impact others and encourage them to find their passion and believe that they too can accomplish greatness. Things once thought impossible, now seem attainable. First, we must find our passion, and then we must live our passion.

Fighting Addiction

Addiction has always intrigued me. I often watch shows that focus on the psyche of addicted individuals. The A&E Channel's, *Intervention,* was one of the programs I frequently watched. The show's premise follows the struggles experienced by individuals addicted to street and/or prescription drugs and the impact their behavior has on those who care for and love them as they try to help them overcome their addiction. Family and/or friends intervene on behalf of the addict; trying to persuade the individual to seek treatment and break free from the addiction. There are myriad underlying causes of addiction, but what most of the individuals have in common is the idea that self-medicating will suppress the underlying problem.

According to the Center for Disease Control (CDC), in 2016, 48.5 million Americans used illicit drugs or misused prescription drugs; with the highest rate of illicit use occurring among those aged 18 to 25. Addiction in the United States is a major health crisis; destroying lives, tearing families apart, and overwhelming the health care system. It has the power to take control of a person's entire life; mind, body, and soul. Until recently, one of my best kept secrets was my drug addiction.

Growing up I often heard the expression, "Too much of anything is bad." I am not sure this applies to all situations, but it was definitely true for me.

My drugs of choice were marijuana and alcohol. As a teenager and young adult, I was exposed to alcohol and marijuana use by friends and acquaintances. Because I wanted to fit in, when I was with these friends, I too would smoke a joint and consume alcohol. Without warning, my drug usage occurred more frequently. When I felt depressed or during times when life seemed meaningless, I smoked a joint or took a drink. It never occurred to me that I was becoming or had become addicted. I had everything under control or so I thought. Other people had addictions, not me! During this phase, I gave no thought to the harm I was doing to my body, nor did I consider the negative impact my seemingly harmless actions would have on my family.

In middle school and through my junior year of high school, I played both football and basketball. In my senior year of high school, I dropped basketball and focused entirely on football. Like thousands of other young athletes, I had dreams of playing for a ranked college team, followed by being drafted by the National Football League or the National Basketball Association. My aspiration was not primarily to make millions of dollars, I simply wanted validation based on my athletic ability. I dedicated so much time and effort to improving my skill level that I did not know who I was outside of these sports. I had never entertained the thought of what my life would be without playing either basketball or football. The summer before my senior year of high school, I turned my entire focus to football and was rewarded with intense recruitment by several major universities. Ultimately, I made the decision to attend Louisiana State University (LSU); my dream school since the days of Shaquille O'Neal.

I arrived in Baton Rouge, LA excited to be a student-athlete on the LSU football team; a Power 5 football institution where each year a number of players were drafted by the NFL. I played on a team with outstanding athletes, including Tyrann Mathieu, Bennie Logan, Michael Brockers, Markevious Mingo, Patrick Peterson, Kelvin Sheppard, Odell Beckham, and Jarvis Landry, to name a few. The team was loaded with talent, and even the least-talented players had an opportunity to make it to the next level. As a freshman on a team with so much talent, I received limited playing time in a few games. I was living my dream, but like waking up in the morning from a deep sleep, reality is altogether different.

I experienced knee troubles dating back to my earlier years playing basketball in high school. When I would complain to the trainer regarding the pain I was experiencing with my knees, he dismissed it as tendonitis. Intuitively, I knew it was something more. During my college sophomore year, I had an experience that significantly changed my life for the worst, or so I thought at the time. I was a redshirt-sophomore, training hard and anticipating a breakout season on the football team. As a means of keeping in shape during the summer, football players would often go to the university's recreational center to play basketball. During this particular workout session, with the ball in hand, I ran to the rim, made a slight jump, and as I did, I heard a loud pop. The unthinkable happened. When I looked down, my kneecap was halfway up my thigh. This undoubtedly was one of the most frightening experiences of my life. It looked so horrendous that I was more focused on the way my knee looked, as opposed to the pain I was experiencing.

My teammates literally carried me to my apartment and called our athletic trainer, who immediately came and took me to the hospital. The tests and X-Ray's reveled that I had more than tendonitis. My tendon had been torn for several months and each day the tendon tear got thinner and thinner until it just completely snapped. The diagnosis was a torn patella tendon on the left kneecap; an injury that usually takes 9-12 months to heal. It was difficult to face the reality of not being able to play immediately. The best way for me to describe the feeling was akin to losing your closest loved one in a tragic incident. I had lost my best friend, the best friend I never thought of living life without and for several days I was numb and in shock. I called my family with the diagnosis and gave them information on the surgery that I would undergo. Though my teammates and coaches were supportive, they were preparing to move on without me. As they should! Talk about going through an emotional roller coaster.

As I processed the pending surgery and the impact it would have on my future, one of my best friends, Joe Hollins and his family prayed for me during their church worship services. It was a powerful prayer. One that called on God for healing and a speedy recovery. At that moment in time I did not believe in prayer, or much of anything. I was shocked, hurt, and disappointed— no hope in sight. The day I went into surgery, my mother and father and their spouses were with me in the hospital. Joe and his family also came and brought me one of my favorite dishes; Pastor Shelly's homemade chicken potpie. It was painfully obvious and extremely unsettling that none of my teammates or coaches came to visit. The people I spent a majority of my time with and saw everyday were not there when I went into the hospital for surgery, came out of the hospital, or went back to my apartment after surgery.

The day after surgery, my parents left to go back to their respective homes. I was now completely alone. In complete solitude with no one to confide in, nothing to do, no viable way to release my frustrations, nowhere to put my energy, and no identity. I was forced to look at myself for who I was and quickly concluded that I was not anything or anyone. Imagine the depression that ensues after coming to that conclusion. But these were the thoughts I struggled with every day for months. While my teammates attended class, practiced together, or hung out; I went to class and afterwards I was locked alone in my apartment for hours and hours.

This depression and isolation led me to heavy drug use. Prior to my injury, I only considered myself a user of marijuana. I would frequently use marijuana and just hide the fact I was doing so. I hid it from my family because I knew they would freak out, from my coaches because I knew it was illegal, and I even hid it from certain groups of friends because I feared they would judge me. For me it was just marijuana. After my injury, my drug use escalated. I was prescribed

Hydrocodone and Percocet; two powerful and very addictive opioids. Team doctors gave me a bottle of both and told me to take one in the morning and one at night. I followed doctors' orders; too well I suppose. My knee was healing, but because I was abusing the pain killers, I now had other more serious problems.

I was forced to out myself and face the music. Nearing the end of my rehabilitation, I began working on running and gaining my strength back, but I still needed the pills to cope. I realized the doctors were monitoring my rehabilitation and continually decreasing the amount of medication I was receiving. I needed to take matters into my own hands to make up the deficit. I increased my dependency on marijuana and identified an individual who purchased prescription drugs for me off the street. I was buying more and more pills and had jars hidden in my room filled with marijuana. It was an expensive habit to say the least, but I knew people who could get me a good deal.

Over time, I experienced the power these pills had to take away pain; not just the bodily pain but the mental and psychological pain. They numbed everything and, if only for a brief period, gave me the feeling of being in a space where I did not have to think about life. I went from taking the prescribed dosage of one pill in the morning and one at night, to taking two of each in the morning and two of each at night. Soon it was a couple at lunch time and before long a couple every hour. This along with my continued alcohol and marijuana usage made my life very intense and frightening. I attributed these feelings to the fear of honestly acknowledging to myself, as well as family and friends, that I was in a deep depression. Finally, it was acknowledged that, I was addicted to more than just the drugs; I was addicted to the feeling of freedom that these drugs provided. It was doing this period that two major life changing moments occurred back-to-back.

I had recently completed rehabilitation treatment on my knee when one early afternoon the football team was preparing for a scrimmage during spring ball. Not wanting to stay and watch my team scrimmage, I went to my apartment. It was difficult for me to watch the team play, especially without knowing if or when I would ever touch the ball again. When I arrived to my apartment, I turned on some music, took a couple of Percocets, and smoked a Black & Mild cigar; now a part of my new normal routine. When the Percocet kicked into my system, I laid down and feel asleep. After my nap, I woke up in an emotional whirlwind; crying and experiencing alternating emotions of numbness, happiness and sadness. I was crying profusely, but I had no explanation for the crying. I was terribly frightened, and uncertain as to what was happening to me. The only thing that came to mind was to call my father in Memphis.

"Daddy," I said, "I am crying but I don't know why I am crying. I don't know what is wrong with me." Without asking any questions, he calmly remarked, "Justin, in life you go through things but the way to handle them is not by using drugs. I remember when your uncle had trouble with certain drugs that caused him many problems in his life. Caused him to not be himself; to be an addict. Your uncle would frequently tell me to never do them, even though I was sitting there watching him using. So, be careful with what you're doing and take care of yourself. You have our support no matter what you're going through. Now fix yourself up and get it together. We love you."

As I listened to his words, I was confused and on high alert. I had never told him I was doing drugs, or that I was struggling mentally. Intellectually, I knew I needed to get it together but I did not know how to begin the process. Mentally, because of my fears, I honestly did not want to get it together. There was the embarrassment and the fear that no one would understand what I was going through; compounded by the fear of losing everything I worked for. There was that fear of not becoming my own man and not just somebody who was hiding behind the identity of my family, city, and sport.

My life slowly started unravelling on a Sunday morning. It was a normal Sunday when the team usually had the day off after playing a Saturday game. My only obligation was an hour tutoring session that began at 5:30 p.m. I remember going to tutoring and dreading every minute of it. All I looked forward to was returning to my apartment so I could smoke and pop a couple of pills. Regardless of what I was doing, always in the back of my mind was the lingering question of when I could get high again. I felt that was the way to suppress the pain and anguish I was experiencing.

Walking back to my apartment after the tutoring session, to my surprise the campus police were there speaking with my roommate. Their reason for the visit was the strong scent of marijuana they smelled coming from our apartment. Inwardly, I panicked as I tried to remain outwardly calm. The police officers left us with this warning: "This is your last chance to get rid of the marijuana, or next time we will be forced to search the apartment and report it to the campus police and athletic department. You are good this time but please get yourselves together." After hearing the police warning, my roommate and I thought we were safe and free to go about our lives as usual. We had dodged the bullet, or so we thought.

On Monday mornings, the football team had 6 a.m. weight-lifting and conditioning. As was customary, I walked into the workout gym and went to my locker on which was attached a note to immediately report to the training room. I was advised that I would not be able to practice, workout, or leave the facilities until I took a mandatory drug test. I thought, "Are you serious?" I had no way out, the only option was failure. Immediately after taking the drug test I called my mother with the news that I had taken a drug test which I could possibly fail; however, I did not admit to smoking marijuana. There was no way I could even bring this up to my father, knowing how disappointed he would be. A couple of days passed before I received the expected phone call. I was told to report to, Les Miles, office. We had about a 30-minute conversation which entailed him telling me I failed a drug test. He also asked me a series of hard questions. "What should I do with you? Should I keep you on the team? Should I suspend you? What will your parents think?" All these were questions I struggled answering under pressure. I said, "Coach, I am sorry. I made a mistake and it won't happen again."

He then told me to go to Coach Frank Wilson's office, where I knew the conversation would be much more intense.

Coach Frank sat me down and asked me the same questions as Coach Miles. In addition, he ran down my current rap sheet since becoming a member of the team: 1) Below average grade; 2) multiple injuries; 3) African-American; 4) limited playing experience; 5) from Memphis, Tennessee; not from the home state of Louisiana; 6) failed drug test.

He asked, "Why should we keep you? From what I just read from this list we have no reason to let you be a part of this team. But we are going to keep you because we see something in you, Justin. We will have to call your family and let them know you failed." He immediately called my father and mother, both of whom were surprised and angry. The very next day my father was on LSU's campus. My parents told other family members and eventually friends and acquaintances learned of my situation. This was the highest level of embarrassment and humiliation that I had ever experienced.

It was a tough couple of weeks to say the least, but I learned first-hand how my decisions affected others and how I could have easily lost it all. In many ways, I had lost it all, but this experience helped me get back on the right path. I recalled the TV show *Scared Straight.* The show's premise was to rehabilitate teenagers who were engaged in destructive activities. Some of the teens had been involved in robberies, sexual activity, fighting, or drugs; sometimes all of the above. They were made to spend 2 days in a prison, in the same environment as inmates, some of whom were serving life sentences.

The inmates are allowed to talk to the teens in the worst way possible while also providing them sound advice; many times, the inmates attempt to create an environment of extreme fear in the teenager. This supposedly causes them to be scared straight; meaning when they leave, they are so scared of the thought of being trapped in jail, they change their behavior and act appropriately and act in a lawful manner. This is what happened to me.

Suffering a career debilitating injury was strike one and using drugs to self-medicate was strike two. Failing the drug test with the possibility of being dismissed from the team and school, with the ensuing embarrassment it would cause my family and others who knew me, was strike three. I had run through the cycle. I realized that I had a problem and that if I did not turn my life around soon then I was headed for destruction. This was the wakeup call I needed. Many times, when dealing with adversity one needs to not just experience hard times but needs to hit rock bottom. I had reached my lowest point; time to start building me back up. Addiction had forced me down a seemingly endless, dark tunnel with no light. Only I was to blame, I was complicit in my own destruction. Once I faced the gravity of what I had done, I realized making the people who were close to me proud was more important to me than the problems I was navigating. It was more important than the numbness I experienced when I was on drugs.

There are different degrees of happiness; self-gratification among them, but I am most fulfilled when I can share my joy and the story of how God tested me and helped me cope with my depression. After coming face-to-face with my addiction and dealing with my demons, my self-esteem increased and I was happier than I had been in a very long time. It is still amazing to me that even when in the deep throes of depression, God helped me discover my true identity and purpose in life—to share with others, especially young people, my story of prospering through adversity. I struggled through the storm, but along the way I glimpsed the bright sunshine. My struggles became my blessings and I now have the HUSTLE of *Having Unlimited Success Through Life-changing Experiences!*

Made In Memphis

I love my hometown, Memphis, Tennessee, located in the western part of the state, bordering the states of Mississippi and Arkansas. Memphis is a gritty, hardworking city and that is reflected in the attitude of its residents. This same attitude is evidenced by the professional Basketball team, Memphis Grizzlies, who play home games in the Grind House, the nickname for the FedEx Forum. Their style of play is representative of the citizens of Memphis, most of whom wake up mornings willing to do the work (grind) it takes to provide for themselves and their families. We are not just talking about people who work normal shifts, but also the hustlers; people who make it in spite of the odds they may face, including unemployment and/or under employment. If you were to ask someone to describe Memphis, you would probably receive a different perspective from each person asked.

I recall coming home in 2014 from LSU for a short weekend visit. My stepfather, Pechone Love, asked me to take a ride with him. I had no idea where we were going, I was just along for the ride; having a men's day out. We ended up in a section of town known as North Memphis, along the way stopping to get haircuts, shopping for clothes and eating dinner. This drive was a bit different from other drives we had taken together around the city. As we drove around town, we listened to Memphis rap legends 8 Ball & MJG, Three-Six Mafia, and Yo Gotti.

We discussed growing up in Memphis and as Pechone reminisced about his youth and his current status, he remarked; "Man I love Memphis and I want you to remember your love for Memphis. It's a special place. I know you plan to travel and live all over the world. That's great! I know you will do well no matter where you are because of your background and the way you are made. If you can make it here, you can make it everywhere. It is something about someone from Memphis that's different from everyone else. We have a certain swagger; You know? We are hustlers. We make it happen by any means. Not because we want to, but because we have too. It's a way of life. Just look around us."

I thought about his statement, and as we continued to drive, I began to intently focus and study the movement of the city and the people we saw. In South Memphis, I noticed an older gentleman on a corner barbecuing on a makeshift grill attached to his truck and selling barbecue plates for $5. In another area of town, a group of men repairing the roof of what appeared to be an old abandoned house caught my attention. In the yard were several old cars which appeared to have been sitting in the same spot for years. In another part of Memphis, a lady was having a vintage yard sale; while waiting for customers she picked and trimmed flowers in her yard. I saw women engaged in solicitation, workers unloading cargo at FedEx, musical blues groups sitting on Beale Street playing their hearts out waiting for passersby's to make donations as they walked by and so much more. I saw the good and the bad; a city of beautiful, hardworking people living life. I saw Memphis.

I have always had a love for Memphis, where I spent my formative years. On a few occasions, individuals have expressed surprise when they learned I was from Memphis. When meeting new people in other cities, the two things they want to talk about are barbecue and crime; in that order. Yes, Memphis can be tough, but in spite of its flaws it is a great city. Most citizens are caring, compassionate, hardworking individuals who are neighborly and willing to help others. A friend from Memphis is a friend for a lifetime.

My best friend, Ferious, is that typical Memphian. I am talking about one of those best friends who was the brother I never had; if you saw me, you saw him. Ferious and I met the summer before our freshman year of high school. If you are wondering how he got his name, it was from his mom. The story is that when she was in labor with him in the hospital, she was watching the movie, *Boyz in the Hood*, who featured a character named Furious. In the movie, Furious was a man full of wisdom, truth, and understanding, which are traits my friend possesses.

We had so much in common. Both of our mothers were single mothers a majority of our lives and they too became good friends. We did nearly everything together from getting girls, cooking at his house, shopping, smoking; we always kept it real. He is my friend; my brother for life and one of only a few males I fully trust till this day. We both had a sense of curiosity and a yearning to learn more. Ferious is a major key to a lot of my success. I referred to him as my "humbling board." Whenever I reached a state of mind where I thought I was the best at what I was doing, he kept me grounded with a reality check. As I state in a previous chapter, I have often battled with a lack of self-confidence; the thought of not being good enough in a particular area. Yet, when I was around Ferious, what he saw was a confident, cocky individual. In high school I received recognition as one of the best players in Tennessee; ranked as the number 1 linebacker in the state and the number 2 best player behind quarterback Barry Burnetti.

I remember times when Ferious and I would talk about upcoming football games and opposing players. It was hilarious because anytime I would ask him who were the top players in our school, city, or state he would never have me on his list. "Really," I asked. "Is that how you feel?" Out of kindness for his friend, I thought he would at least put me in the middle of his Top 5 list of outstanding players. He would give me a serious look and say, "You are all right, but you are not all that bro. Let's just say that you got some stuff you need to do." I would be irritated by his remarks, but in all seriousness, when I think about it, he was right. I did have a lot to work on and I instinctively knew he was right because I would repeatedly hear his voice in the back of my head saying this for the remainder of my football career.

Ferious was, and still is, my humbling board. He is the person who reminds me that no matter how good I think I am, there is that need to continue to get better. When striving to be our best, we may often think our success is attributable to our skills and abilities. A lack of humility can be a major stumbling block to success. This is why we all need a Ferious, that trustworthy person who out of love and concern speaks truth to us even when we do not want to hear the truth. Whenever we talk, Ferious and I reminisce about high school and the good times we had, but his list of outstanding high school players from our era still does not include me.

After writing this chapter of the book, I called Ferious to tell him how he was an integral part of my success. To my surprise, he opened up and shared the following: "I did not idolize you like most did. I just saw you as my boy, my brother. We were the same so, I didn't see you in that light. I knew you were great and talented. I saw the small hometown fame eat at you and I didn't want to keep that pressure up. We were boys. We didn't have to fake it to make it.

He continued, "Most guys were just trying to ride your coat tail to get their recruiting done. You put us on the map when you went to those camps and started getting this attention. Before you, we might have had a couple get recruited but nobody was really getting put on until you started the trend. This is where your legend lies, it lies in helping people take that next step. I never realized how many steps ahead of us you were, but with the immaturity we hung around with, I'm glad we prevailed." Our relationship is a testament to our upbringing in Memphis, a testament to our friendship and loyalty, the values instilled in us by parents, family, friends, coaches, and others.

The Truth

I have been asked me why I chose football over basketball and I laughingly say, Tarik Black. A power forward currently playing in the Euro League, he has played for the Los Angeles Lakers and the Houston Rockets. Hands down, he is one of the hardest working and most humble people I know. We met in 2010 as freshmen at Ridgeway High School where we both played on the basketball team. We were the big men in the post and during practice would go head-to-head on the court. Because of my prior basketball experience, I remember the first few weeks of the season handling Tarik pretty well, but towards the middle of the season something changed. He was getting better, going from barely getting rebounds, not blocking shots, and missing layups to actually coming down with a few rebounds and blocking a couple shots. He was blocking my shots at practice!

At this point, I saw my basketball career diminishing. Tarik had decided he was going to be the best basketball player he could be; not knowing if that was going to make him the best player in the city, the best player in the state, or the best player in the country. He just wanted to be the best he could be, not only for himself, but for his family and others who believed in him. Before the end of the season, Tarik was a starter on the team. The next year, he had a breakout season on the team that won the Boys' State Championship.

Tarik then went on to be one of the best players in the country, receiving multiple scholarship offers before deciding to play for the University of Memphis where he received his Bachelor's Degree and transferring to the University of Kansas where he received his Master's Degree. Tarik is a success in every sense of the word and is an example of the Memphis Hustle.

On March 1, 2018, I woke up to an alert on my phone notifying me of an article about Tarik titled, *NBA Star Tarik Black Suddenly Got Called into Street Ministry - His Powerful Prayer for This Woman Was Perfect.* I read the title I nodded my head and said, "That sounds like Tarik." As I continued to read the inspiring and uplifting article, I realized how special Tarik is. This man is more than just a basketball success; he is a life success. The woman he prayed for was a homeless lady on the street who did not want money from him—she did not know who he was—she stated she needed Jesus. Tarik and his friend formed a circle around the woman and he began to pray for her. Afterwards, she was invited to join the group for dinner.

These anecdotes about Pechone, Ferious, and Tarik illustrate the character of many Memphians. They include those who raised me to be the man I am today and to those who were instrumental in instilling within me a sense of pride in the city of my birth. Most of us are familiar with the phrase, "Home is where the heart is." Memphis will always be where my heart lies; it is the home of HUSTLE where one's blank slate can become a beautiful work of art.

To Memphis; Home of the Blues, Beale Street, Elvis Presley, National Civil Rights Museum, largest African-American population in Tennessee, World Championship Barbecue Contest, I say: "Thank you." To my father, who has made it his life's goal to build and develop Memphis through his real estate efforts and joint ventures, "Thank you." To my family and friends who love and support me unconditionally, "Thank you." To everyone in the 901, "Thank you."

Education Helps Expression

As a very young child, one of the things we are constantly told is how important it is to learn and receive a quality education. At 2 or 3 years of age, children may be given blocks shaped like triangles, squares, and circles to begin the process of differentiating between shapes, learn socialization and language skills, memorize the alphabet and how to count, and engage in activities to develop motor skills. Then there is pre-K, kindergarten, and on and on. Education is a continuous process that prepares us for a life of learning and adaptation.

HUSTLE (Having Unlimited Success Through Life-changing Events) is difficult without the ability to express and apply what has been learned. This came to mind when I was speaking to a group of young adults and community leaders at the closing ceremony for Education Equals Opportunity Too (E=O2). The organization's mission is to socially and academically influence, impact, motivate, and positively influence at risk youth by instilling in them the concept that education equals opportunity. During the ceremony, students who have successfully completed the program are awarded a laptop computer, printer, and backpack for their transition to high school or college.

What impressed me most were the children who spoke about the program and their personal goals. It was interesting to hear about their personal lives, educational experiences, and ideas on how they planned to impact the world. Their speeches were so touching and authentic that when I looked down at my notes for my prepared speech, I decided I had to speak from the heart and trash my prepared speech.

I went on stage and thanked my good friend, Walter Larkins and his wife, for allowing me to be a part of the E=O2 family. I immediately launched into my speech by reflecting on my life and the journey that brought me to that place in time. I spoke of how programs similar to E=O2 contributed to my successes and why they are so desperately important. I grew up in a family of educators. My late grandfather was a renowned teacher and principal in the Memphis City School District, my grandmother and great aunt are retired teachers, my cousin Vickie is also a teacher. Before becoming a principal my mother was a teacher and an assistant principal. She has received numerous awards for her leadership skills and is currently working on her Ph.D. degree.

My mother was the first person who taught me that education provides the tools that allows one to express thoughts and ideas. Most parents constantly reinforce the importance of a quality education and the opportunities that it provides with their children. My mother was no different, except she took it to another level when I was in elementary school. In the fifth grade I attended Ross Elementary school, a predominately African-American school in a middle-class suburban neighborhood. It was also the school where my mother taught fifth grade.

I fondly remember the principal, Dr. Roderick Richmond, whom I admired. He was confident and professional in his demeanor and dress, and my mother always spoke so highly of him. Ross Elementary was a great school where I met people I now call family; particularly Mrs. Katika Davis and her three children. Mrs. Davis took care of me during those times when my mother had to work late or had other activities that required a "babysitter." I could literally write a whole section about how she impacted my life. I called her my godmother because that is what she felt like to me.

In fifth grade, I was blessed with the opportunity to be assigned to my mother's class. Students were assigned two teachers throughout the school day, to get them acclimated to changing classes the following year in middle school. I had Mrs. Bradford for math and science and my mother for English and spelling. When I first learned my mother would be my teacher, I had mixed emotions; happy because I was a momma's boy and loved being around my mother, but I was also hesitant because everyone knew I was a momma's boy. Either I was going to get special treatment other students would not receive, or I was going to get embarrassed because of the things I was not doing. Needless to say, all of the above happened.

While in my mother's class, I believe I had the most positive experiences of my educational career. It was not because of the subject matter she taught, but because she provided opportunities for students to express themselves. To teach the structure of writing a five-paragraph paper, every week students were given an assignment to write about anything they wished. What made this so special was that most of the students chose to write about their life experiences.

After writing for approximately 90 minutes, each student had to stand in front of the class and either read their story or share its contents. This was the beginning of my hidden love for writing and expression. One of the things many people never knew about me was that I loved to write. I have notebooks from high school and college with random raps and poems that I would share with only a few people. When I go back and read them, I feel brilliant and embarrassed at the same time. Whenever I write, I reflect back on my experiences in my mother's fifth-grade class. One of the first poems I wrote in college is titled, *Have You?* I feel now is the perfect time to share it.

Have You?

Have you ever felt unseen?

Have you ever felt invisible?

Have you ever felt seen through?

Have you ever been in a room full of people and been the life of the party and still feel alone?

Have you ever just thought, "Why am I here?"

Have you ever not had the answer to that question?

Have you?

Have you ever asked yourself; "Why is there nobody here who looks like me?

Have you ever asked yourself, "Why am I in this safe environment and feel like I'm in danger when in all rationality everyone sees me as the main threat?"

Have you ever asked, "Why am I the threat? I sit because of my intelligence, my smartness, my above average good looks?"

Have you ever just said, "Maybe I should be what they assume me to be?" But no, what do I look like lowering my standards to theirs?

Sure you have. I know you have. Talk about being black in America,

where doing right and being polite can still leave you a victim of dislike

and spite.

Oh well, that's life. I'm still going to shine and trust me it's hard, but I

am about that life. I'm not going out without a fight.

This poem was one of my first and when I think about it, it was ahead of its time considering all the strife and conflict African Americans are having in this country. What I found was expression allows you to educate yourself while allowing you to be put in an uncomfortable state of being but when done right you feel free.

I often do research on people who I deem to be prolific in their approach to life and when you dig deep into who they are they all are just using their education to express the thoughts they've had stored inside of them their entire life. One of my favorite artists is Prince, who passed away in April of 2016. Obviously, music is a source of expression, but, when he passed away, they found thousands of unreleased songs and manuscripts containing his thoughts on love and life. Maybe we can talk about the great Maya Angelou, who was an activist in many ways through her writing. One of my favorites is our first President of the

United States, George Washington, who wrote daily manuscripts about his plans for this country and how God would bless them with an abundance of resources through the process.

I took this approach of learning through expression all through my life without anyone ever knowing because of my shyness and embarrassment about it. When I tell my mom I am a speaker and writer she still asks me, "Where did this come from? You were nothing like this growing up?", when in all rationality I was but just kept it to myself.

Education provides one with tools for communicating thoughts and ideas, written and/or verbal. These skills were particularly critical during my master's program at Louisiana State University where writing papers and essays were a major part of the curriculum. My classmates thought of me as a hard worker and overachiever. This was true because our studies were primarily focused on students' personal opinions regarding current topics in American and Higher Education. My writings were an outlet for me to express my thoughts, in a formal educational setting, on relatively recent higher education topics including race and identity and the transitional phases students faced when coming from a lower economic background, being a first-generation college student, and the overall understanding of how to navigate college campus when being underrepresented. Because of my upbringing and background, I could relate to the research topic and upon awaking each morning I looked forward to proving my belief that an athletes' successful collegiate scholastic achievement was dependent on a quality high school education which included being able to effectively communicate. When speaking to groups, I emphasize using education as a vehicle to self-expression and to not think of learning as a chore or an inconvenience.

As a student-athlete, I had a particular interest in identifying the percentage of athletes who did not complete a four-year degree program, or if they did, the percentage of those who did not pursue a post-graduate degree. Because of my experiences as a student-athlete, in classroom discussions and one-on-one dialogue I often found myself attempting to dismiss pre-conceived notions of athletes focusing primarily on their sport, as opposed to academics; particularly African-Americans athletes. Dr. Jennifer Curry, one of my master's professors, afforded me the opportunity to work with her on a study on graduation rates among this group with the intent to provide more than just anecdotal information.

Dr. Curry and I discussed my interest in college athletes and my interest in identifying ways to be of help to them in completing their degree requirements; ultimately leading to graduation. Though my career in college athletics is relatively short, I have already developed a philosophy which drives my ambition and passion for what I do. My goal in the research study was to identify factors that contribute to student-athletes often leaving college before graduating. Dr. Curry asked me to give her my perspective and reasons I thought were factors in athletes not completing a degree program. The list is as follows: 1.) Disparity in funding of men and women sports programs 2.) Student-athletes in revenue driven sports not being compensated for their performance 3.) Identification of inclusive environments 4.) Student-athletes' college readiness 5.) Student-athletes' mental health 6). University assisted navigation of a student-athlete's academic experience

The concern that caught Dr. Curry's attention was student-athletes' college readiness. She asked if I were interested in doing a study on African-American student-athletes high school experiences in preparation for college preparedness and their subsequent success. Because I'd had numerous classroom discussions on the subject, in addition to submitting papers on the same topic, I immediately accepted the invitation to help conduct the research. It only made sense for me to do this study and validate my previously held beliefs.

My Belief:

"African American male athletes are a unique and marginalized

population in Higher Education; they are less likely than their white,

male counterparts, female athletes, and collegiate non-athlete peers to be

successful academically and in their postsecondary careers (Vereen, Hill,

Lopez, 2015). However, the trajectory of educational problems for

African American male athletes begins well before their postsecondary

experience. Indeed, much of the academic and career outcomes at the

collegiate level may be attributed to K-12 educational preparation.

Assisting in the research was Dr. Curry's graduate assistant,

Sammy Latham. The qualitative study surveyed the LSU football team

whose demographics were 60% African-American; 30% Caucasian; and

10% other. The survey questions were designed to elicit information on

the athletes' academic preparation for post-secondary education. African-

American players responded that they had an ineffective high school

experience that included a lack of college preparatory classes, a school

climate where education was not perceived as highly valued, few if any

academic tutors, limited teaching/learning supplies, and single-parent

households. Most of the same conditions existed in the Hispanic and

Asian Pacific Islander population. The Caucasian players' unanimous results indicated that the schools they had attended offered college preparatory and AP classes and adequate teaching tools. Most of the players came from two-parent homes and primarily lived in middle or upper middle-class, suburban neighborhoods.

We also conducted interviews with four of the students, whose oral responses reflected the findings of the qualitative study. The study titled *African American Male Collegiate Athletes' Perceptions of Their Career and Academic Preparation* was later published in an academic journal, revealing that African-American players were usually on full scholarship and majored in General Studies or Sports Management. Many of the Caucasian players were walk-ons who received no financial assistance, and many of whom were enrolled in the Engineering or Business Schools. My participation in this study was an example of how education leads to expression and credibility.

More importantly, my thoughts which I had often expressed in my writings were validated and have strongly influenced my career and life goals. I urge individuals to express their opinions and thoughts on issues of interest and concern to them; however, before doing so, be curious enough to do the research to lend credibility to those expressions.

This is HUSTLE; Having Unlimited SuccessThrough Life-changing Experiences!

LSU

College of

Human Sciences & Education

School of Education

African American Male Collegiate Athletes' Perceptions Of Their Career and Academic Preparation

Justin Maclin • Samantha J. Latham

Louisiana State University

School of Education • Baton Rouge, LA 70803

1. Challenge/Issue

African American male athletes are a unique and marginalized population in higher Education, they are less likely than their white counterparts, female athletes, and collegiate nonathlete peers to be successful academically and in their post-graduate careers (Vanum, Hill, & Logue, 2015). However, the majority of educational programs for African American athletes begin to yield the academic and career success of the students in these programs. (Much of the scholarly literature on the experiences and practices of these students may be attributed to K-12 educational preparation.

2. Social Capital Framework

First conceptualized by Bourdieu (1986), social capital is defined as the aggregate of the actual or potential resources which are linked to possession of a durable network of more or less institutionalized relationships of mutual acquaintance and recognition (p. 248). In other words, the social network that an individual belongs to gives them access to the group's overall resources and opportunities.

The social capital framework presents students, each as a peer group or formal network. Social capital is manifested in the following breakdown: 18 freshmen, 16 sophomores, 9 juniors, 8 seniors, and 2 graduate students.

3. Social Capital for College

College access and college readiness resources are important when first becoming a family member-informed college going or family member-informed college students such as having access to college application framework, using college websites, and knowing how to apply to college and understanding college going websites align to degrees and costs of major, and developing financial literacy

4. Mixed Methods

Research Questions:

(1) What programs are developed at the institution for student-athletes to promote academic growth and life maturity?

(2) Do athletes contribute to, or create barriers to, individual's academic and career development? In what ways?

(3) How do the student-athletes view their academic growth and development prior to coming to college?

(4) What consequences, positive or negative, do they attribute to their pre-college academic preparation?

Data Collection and Analysis

The data described was collected from self-reported questionnaires given to a university's football team at a research intensive university in the Southeastern Conference. In addition, we conducted three interviews with participants chosen with unique outcomes. The data was interpreted through a phenomenological perspective and emphasis on career and college readiness.

5. Participants

Survey Participants:

Participants were 53 student athletes on a Division 1 football team at a large university in the southeastern United States. All participants were male and the ages ranged from 17 years to 26 years, with the average being 20 years of age. Of the 53 players surveyed, 37 identified as African American/Black and 16 identified as White, non-Hispanic. There were representatives from each classification level, with the following breakdown: 18 freshmen, 16 sophomores, 9 juniors, 8 seniors, and 2 graduate students.

Interview Participants:

Participant 1 (JR) is an African American walk-on collegiate football player. He is a 21-year-old junior majoring in Sports Administration, with a concentration in Sport Leadership. He plans on going to the military when he graduates although he is not currently active in ROTC. He noted that he does not know of any other career path so he is choosing the military due to uncertainty. Participant 2 (JD), is a White, non-Hispanic, walk-on collegiate football player who has earned a scholarship for the last two years of eligible play. He is a 21-year-old junior majoring in Architecture and plans on being a year-old when he graduates. Participant 3 (FH) is an African American collegiate football player on full scholarship. He is a 22, and is majoring in Interdisciplinary Studies. He has a 3-year-old daughter who lives with him while he is in school. He plans on being a teacher when he graduates, but his degree will not certify him for his intended career path.

6. Results: First-Generation Students

Table 1.

First-Generation status by Race		
	Yes (N%)	No (N%)
African American	13 (24.5%)	24 (45.3%)
White	0 (0.0%)	16 (30.2%)
Total	13 (24.5%)	40 (75.5%)

Table 2.

Responses to Career and College Readiness Questions

7. Results: Career and College Readiness Preparation

Survey Question	Responded: Yes (N%/N,%*%), to the prompt	Responded: No (N%/N,%*%), to the prompt	Responded: Unsure (N%/N,%*%), to the prompt
While in high school, I was pushed to take as many honors and Advanced Placement (AP) courses as I could handle taking.	27 (50.9%)* 14 (26.4%) 13 (24.5%)	26 (49.1%)* 23 (43.4%) 3 (5.7%)	0 (0.0%) 0 (0.0%) 0 (0.0%)
I met at least once teacher tell me about a career outside of athletics that I might enjoy and have an aptitude for.	37 (69.8%) 22 (41.5%) 15 (28.3%)	16 (30.2%) 15 (28.3%) 1 (1.9%)	0 (0.0%) 0 (0.0%) 0 (0.0%)
While in high school I had the opportunity to participate in extracurricular research or learning activities (such as robotics team, debate team, 4H).	38 (71.7%) 24 (45.3%) 14 (26.4%)	6 (11.3%) 5 (9.4%) 1 (1.9%)	9 (17.0%) 8 (15.1%) 1 (1.9%)
I had opportunities to explore career options through my high school curriculum so that I was certain to choose a degree program in college that fit my future career plans.	10 (18.9%) 7 (13.2%) 3 (5.7%)	43 (81.1%) 30 (56.6%) 13 (24.5%)	0 (0.0%) 0 (0.0%) 0 (0.0%)
Although I knew I would potentially qualify for an athletic scholarship, someone at my high school still explained to me how to apply for academic, merit, or need based scholarships.	39 (73.6%) 26 (49.1%) 13 (24.5%)	14 (26.4%) 11 (20.8%) 3 (5.7%)	0 (0.0%) 0 (0.0%) 0 (0.0%)
	42 (79.2%) 28 (52.8%) 14 (26.4%)	11 (20.8%) 9 (17.0%) 2 (3.8%)	0 (0.0%) 0 (0.0%) 0 (0.0%)

Note. N = total number of African American participants. N* = total number of White participants. *Of the 37 participants who responded "Yes" to the question "While in high school, I was pushed to take as many honors and Advanced Placement (AP) courses as I could handle taking" only 22 reported taking advanced courses. *Of the 38 participants who responded "No" to the same question, 4 reported taking advanced classes.

8. Findings

Because this study is in preliminary analysis, we do not have completed findings, but we do know all of the football players who participated in the study have dramatic differences in their academic histories and upbringing. For example, some football players were told by their high school teachers to think about other possible occupations, to take advances courses, to focus on standardized testing, and to think about their lives outside of athletics. However, the majority of the African American athletes in this sample were not taught or offered the same advice because of low family, career and college readiness capital. High athletic recruitment, and low academic focus at their high school. As we explored different areas (i.e. African Americans received less information on academic rigor and career development). Sample statements from the phenomenology interviews are given below. The first two are from African American participants (majoring in interdisciplinary studies and sports administration), the third a White participant (architecture major).

Researcher: Were you pushed to take minimum required courses to graduate high school or honors courses?

FH: No, we only took minimum required courses.

Researcher: How would you have prepared differently while in high school?

JR: I would have pursued a career such as being a vet if I had more time to focus on academics rather than sports.

Researcher: Are you able to finish your education while playing football?

JD: No, internships are not possible because the summer course I have to take prevents me from having time during those months to do an internship when the rest of my classmates do. It puts me at a slight disadvantage and I have through LSU football provide me an equal advantage over my peers.

9. Implications

Despite a lack of adequate career and academic preparation in K-12 student-athletes do have opportunities to make up for these skills while in college if given adequate resources and opportunities. An exemplary resource is the Shaquille O'Neal Life Skills Program. This program focuses on career planning and development, financial literacy, community relations and outreach, and life skills counseling, which fosters a sense of life-long preparedness. Although most universities will not have a Shaquille O'Neal program, incorporating some components, including those that assist athletes for choosing careers that align to college majors, are important to student-athletes who have no opportunity for a career in athletics upon completion of their degree. Additional career development opportunities such as numerous holistic career assessments (i.e. career values, interests, personality, skills) that are then explored to the students would be helpful. Additional components of such a program at a research through college should include resume building, interview skills, and job shadowing days as many athletes miss internship opportunities due to their athletic commitments.

The Game Plan

One of the books I have added to my collection is *Positive Possibilities* by Matthew Jenkins, an author, philanthropist, real estate mogul, and former veterinarian. This inspiring book, a gift from my friend, Marcus, examines how one's mindset and views shape life's possibilities. Many forward-thinking people have an initial plan of action, but when faced with adversity, there is no back-up plan for that unexpected bump in the road. Dr. Jenkins writes of his experiences which illustrate the importance of planning.

Dr. Jenkins received a doctoral degree in veterinary medicine in 1957 from Tuskegee University. While serving in the U. S. Air Force in Greenland, he provided veterinarian services for the large German shepherds used as a first line of defense. Working with the animals, Dr. Jenkins observed that a number of the dogs became ill for no apparent reason and shortly afterwards they would die. Unable to determine the cause of death, he sought permission to conduct a study to seek answers. His findings confirmed his hypothesis that the dogs had rabies. This was a major discovery in that it was thought that rabies did not exist in dogs in Greenland.

Realizing he had made an astonishing and possible career changing discovery, Dr. Jenkins made plans to have his research published. Before he could publish his findings, the doctors he reported to in Greenland claimed they discovered the disease, while giving him only minimal credit. He was understandably angry, but rather than let his anger control him, he created a plan of action. After his discharge, he faced another obstacle; the Air Force reneged on its promise to assign him to California and sent him to a small town in Michigan.

Dr. Jenkins' career was not going exactly as he had envisioned, but rather than wallow in self-pity, he developed another plan of action. While in Michigan, he officially published his study of rabies study in the *Journal of the American Veterinary Medical Association.* The detailed facts he was able to provide discredited the original article for which others had taken major credit. His publication gained national recognition and was a major boost to his career. Though he faced obstacles, his plans of action led him to receive the recognition he had earned.

Using a football analogy, the best time to prepare a backup plan of action, is before the game begins. When I think of creating a game plan, I immediately reflect on my time as a player for the LSU Tigers.

Every year I was on the team, we were ranked among one of the best teams in the country; never ranking outside of the Top 25 teams in college football. In Les Miles, we had the winningest coach in school history. Coach Miles was an amazing coach who prepared the team physically and mentally with the intent to successful compete against and defeat the opposing team, regardless of who they were.

This meant that we relied heavily on our defense to keep us in the game and for our offense to run the ball 75% of the time. Because of our overwhelming talent, this often worked for us. One thing I respected about Coach Miles was his deliberateness in preparing us for victory every day of practice. We never went into a game thinking we were unprepared or that we would lose. Now that I am working in college athletics, I have established relationships with athletes across the country who played for other teams. Those former players have shared their experiences of going into games knowing they were going to not only get battered and bruised, but they were going to leave the stadium in defeat. Thanks to Coach Miles, I never had those feelings of defeat. Before every game, he would come into the locker room and make this speech:

"Gentleman we have practiced long and hard, we have prepared backwards and forwards for our opponent. Do you feel the stadium? Do you hear the fans? They are ready, they are ready to see you perform and impose your will on a team who just doesn't understand the severity of the pain they are about to receive in Death Valley. Every time the ball snaps they will regret they decided to fly to the great city of Baton Rouge. Every time they get up off the beautiful grass of Tiger Stadium, they will know the Tigers are hungry and are hunting for victory. Men, there is no other group I could see myself going to battle with, and I tell you this, after the clock reads zero, they will know. THEY WILL KNOW! Let's go give them what they came to receive; an ass kicking of massive proportions that will end in pools of blood, extreme pain, and death because Tiger Stadium is where our opponent's dreams come to die. MEN TAKE THE FIELD!"

I felt a chill go through my entire while typing this. He would finish his speech and we would charge onto the field like the ancient Spartans going into battle. Coach Miles was a uniquely great motivator who made us believe in ourselves, and also made sure we were prepared as a team. I believe that the one and only thing we struggled with, which I think caused us to not win a championship, was our inability to adjust our game plan. Anytime we lost a game against a formidable opponent, it was because they capitalized on our team's strength, which was running the football.

The most memorable and heartbreaking game loss I experienced was the 2012 National Championship game against University of Alabama. Earlier in the year, we had beaten Alabama in a close game by running the ball and by the defense preventing a touchdown. We went into the championship game with a similar plan only to have Alabama immediately stop everything we attempted to do. We still attempted to run the ball a majority of the time, but we never ended up getting past mid-field. It is something I had never seen anyone do against the Tigers. We had the capability to beat this team by throwing the ball and opening up the offense, but we did not. The defense was on the field too much, and as a result they were fatigued and frustrated. **We lost; 21-0!**

What was the reason for this embarrassing defeat? After the game, sports commentators noted our failure to make adjustments to the game plan once we saw it was not producing a positive outcome. Could ego have been the reason we did not switch up the game plan, or was it an unfailing belief in the game plan and talent we had? Nobody will ever know, but this loss taught me a lesson: Always be ready to adjust your plans because what you think should happen may not happen. Life has its road bumps and obstacles that may cause plans to quickly and unexpectedly change. This is how the philosophy of HUSTLE can be invaluable.

My father, James Maclin, has always drilled into me the importance of having a plan of action and a backup for that plan. Even though I spent a majority of my time growing up with my mother, my father was, and is, a major influence in my life. I still call him when I have questions and concerns, or when I need to make grown up decisions. He is a real estate developer, and often when I go home, he will take me on tours to see development opportunities, like a vacant plot of land or an abandoned apartment complex. He has the uncanny ability to look at these sites and see the potential it has to become something better. After analyzing the potential possibilities, he develops numerous game plans for ways to develop his vision. Not just one game plan, but several. He often shares his decisions with me and the manner in which he reached that decision. His approach to decision making was the tool I needed to become an entrepreneur.

When I lived in Long Beach, I shared with my father a need to increase my financial opportunities working in my chosen career.

California is ranked as one of the Top10 most expensive states to live in the United States; Hawaii being # 1 and California is #2 in 2018 per CNBC.com. To supplement my income, I created Maclin Motivation, LLC, which brought in additional funds from speaking engagements at schools, universities, profit and nonprofit organizations. I also formed a partnership with Ashton Anderson; starting a website design, graphic design, and social media management company, from which I received additional funds. The funds I received from the two business slightly boosted my total income, but the cost of living in Long Beach only marginally improved my finances. My father knew I loved Long Beach and wanted to remain in the area, but he also felt there were better financial opportunities for me in other cities.

"Justin," he said, both of your businesses are things you can do from anywhere. You can take them from city to city with no trouble, so don't worry about those companies because if anything it will only make your market grow bigger. As to your career in college athletics, you are worth way more than what they are willing to pay you. I recommend you apply for other jobs you want; I would even apply for jobs for which you might be slightly over-qualified." He suggested that I test the waters for other opportunities, so as much as I did not want to, I applied for open opportunities at other universities.

"Once you get the offer from a couple of the jobs, present them to your current employer and see if they can match the pay. If not, we will plan from there." Throughout the entire process, my father never made it seem as if I were making these tough decisions on my own; he always made it appear that we were in this together. He was my mental safety blanket in the event things did not go as I planned.

Shortly after we had this discussion, I was more confident as I applied for jobs at universities across the country. The schools that expressed interest in hiring me, offered me at least double the pay and the opportunity to work in the sport area I know best, football. The difficult part was that I really wanted to stay in California, which limited my options. Fortunately, I received calls from two California schools where I had applied for employment, one was UC-Davis where I am currently working. UC-Davis flew me up from Long Beach for an interview and three days later offered me a job; which I accepted.

Of course, I did not want to leave Long Beach, but I had to for financial and career reasons. Since I consider myself a person of integrity, I reached out to individuals in the Long Beach community who had offered friendship and support to let them know I had accepted a position at UC-Davis. I did not want my newfound friends to think I had taken our relationship for granted. I felt the honorable thing to do was to let them know why I was leaving. Many of the people I was most worried about telling were the most supportive. If people really care for you and want you to reach your potential, they will be happy to see you make advances in your career. One of my first donors at Long Beach State and ardent supporter, Stephen Wolfe, called me after receiving the news of my departing the university.

"Justin, I got your message. It saddens Diane and me that you are leaving us, but oddly enough we were talking about you a couple of days ago about how you have so much potential and deserve something better than what you are doing. We were lucky to even snag someone like you for as long as we did. We truly hope the best for you and know you will do great things at your next destination. You always have a home in Long Beach." These sentiments made me feel like my time in Long Beach was well spent and that in my brief stay, I had made a difference.

Within days of accepting the position at UC Davis, I received a call from another university, still in California, that offered more money, responsibility, and a higher visibility. The interview would be scheduled

before beginning my new job at Davis. What should I do? I received

advice from many, some suggesting that I take the interview. I had made

a commitment and was uncomfortable scheduling an interview with

another school. I called a couple of my mentors in the industry whose

opinions I valued. I placed a call to Derek Horne, Director of Athletics at

Alcorn State University, to discuss the job offers, their advantages and

disadvantages, and how each decision could impact my future in the

industry.

I explained that I had accepted the job at UC Davis, but another

school had called with a better financial package. I asked him to go give

me his opinion. Because I never want to miss a potential opportunity, I

may sometimes act too impulsively. Depending on the situation,

impulsiveness can be an asset or a liability. Derek asked me to slow

down and think about my values and how I want to be viewed in the

future by others.

"Which job do you want most?" was his first question. "Which

school has officially offered you the job and which job is the best fit for

you? All signs point to Davis. I know the other one pays a little more,

but are you ready for it? Do you think it would suit you well to interview for it after you have already committed to another place who seems to really value your talent and actively pursued you?

Do they deserve to be treated like the back door? You are young and talented. You will go far in your career no matter which job you take, but word travels fast in this industry and you should always be weary of this. If you're the guy I think you are, I think I know the decision you will make."

I knew I would be going to UC Davis, which was the best choice for me. Many of the problems we worry about can be resolved if we ask ourselves some basic questions. Does this fit into my value system? Does this decision put my integrity in doubt? Will this decision potentially cause regret? When making tough decisions, I always ask myself these questions and because I do, my life is less stressful. It helps me to thoughtfully and carefully evaluate what I should or should not do. It is my blueprint for success through life-changing experiences.

Opening New Doors

Remember the classic cartoon, Scooby-Doo, a show about four teenage friends and their Great Dane (Scooby-Doo) who traveled to and from regular teenage functions in a bright green van solving strange and hilarious mysteries. This show is one of my all-time favorites because even though Scooby-Doo was always afraid and fearful; yet, his fear was one of the factors that allowed him to accidentally solve crimes and achieve hero status.

On one episode, I recall the bad guy entering a space with a wall of doors. The kids had to decide which door was the one entered by the perpetrator. They selected a door and traveled through its corridors without locating the bad guy but finding clues to help solve the mystery. They entered other doors only to discover a list of possible candidates who could possibly be the one responsible for their problems. The final door entered was also empty; the perpetrator had gotten away. However, going through all the doors provided the team with the clues needed to solve the mystery. Using the clues found behind the doors, and with Scooby's assistance, the group was able to eliminate suspects one by one and identify the villain.

This is similar to the experiences I have had opening new doors in my life. Like Scooby-Doo, I have my fears, but I am also excited about the clues I may find behind the door that will assist me in identifying the problem and finding a solution. My route to public speaking took a similar path. Though not considered a public speaker, I had often gone to middle and high schools and shared stories about my life and the importance of college to my success. When I moved to Long Beach, Lesia Buckhalter, invited me to a meeting of the Lakewood Toastmaster Club. I clearly had no idea what Toastmaster was, but I agreed to attend. I learned that Toastmasters is an organization providing opportunities for individuals to work on development and/or improvement of leadership and public speaking skills.

My first "Ice Breaker speech was about my childhood and background. The audience was receptive, and I was honored as the "Best Speaker" for the night. I subsequently joined the club and every week for 2 months, I gave a speech. I was addicted to giving empowering messages to people, while also taking advantage of opportunities to quench my competitive thirst by winning best speaker awards and ultimately competing in the yearly Toastmasters Internationals Competitions.

I eventually shared with my father how much I loved public speaking and that my research revealed that people were handsomely paid for delivering life changing speeches. "Daddy," I asked, "What do you think about me starting a company based on my public speaking?" At this time, I had built up my confidence from the speeches I had given at Toastmasters.

"Make a business plan and go for it," was his response, and I did just that. I went to my office, turned on the computer, and typed out my master plan; including my vision, mission statement, and the services I would offer. I reached out to a close friend and now business partner, Ashton Anderson, a website and graphic designer, to create a company logo website.

My plan was to launch the company after the website was completed which would take approximately 8 weeks. During that time, I arranged small speaking engagements for a portfolio to provide prospective clients with evidence that I was a serious businessman with a service that would benefit, not only me, but also their organization. One of my first clients under Maclin Motivation, LLC, was Long Beach District 3 Councilwoman, Suzie Price. I contacted her office, made an appointment, and over coffee, I told her my plan. Subsequently, she arranged for me to speak to an estimated group of 150 youth about the severity and consequences of bullying and how I dealt with it when I was younger. The group was attentive as they appeared to hang on every word. I knew I was providing a service to others, and I was inspired.

When opening new doors in life, even small victories are appreciated. My joy comes from knowing my words, voice, and story are helping people in their day-to-day lives. Others tell me they cannot do what I do. I simply tell them that everyone's life is different and not all stories are the same, but if we choose, we all have stories we can share with others. You never know how your life's journey can affect or resonate with others, so I encourage you to tell your story if it will help others. Open the door, you may be pleasantly surprised at what is waiting for you on the other side. Do not let fear or failure keep you from your purpose.

I was asked by an elderly gentleman if I knew the richest place on earth. My immediate reply was Dubai. "No," he replied, "It's the cemetery. I was totally baffled and responded with, "What and how?" This had to be a trick question. Then he explained his answer. "Because people die with all their priceless thoughts and ideas. Don't die with your ideas. Put them out there and allow them to manifest into something bigger than you can imagine."

Wise words from a brilliant man that I took to heart. After completing additional speaking engagements, I preceded to promote the business on social media with teasers that I had something major coming. This was me starting to officially crack open the door. To gage how people would respond to the business, I posted to my personal Facebook and LinkedIn accounts pictures of my logo and pictures with motivational quotes. I received numerous feedback from people wanting to see what I had up my sleeve. I was excited, but nervous because I knew there was no turning back. While waiting on the creation of the website and doing speaking engagements, I also created business social media accounts on Twitter, Facebook, and Instagram. Instagram is a social networking app, but I included it in my business model so viewers could be more in touch with me by following my daily life, including my other businesses and career activities. I was employing techniques I had seen used by other successful entrepreneurs.

The Maclin Motivation LLC website, complete with information, videos and pictures was completed on March 25, 2018, and the official launch was scheduled for April 1, 2018. My fears and uncertainty were heightened as I questioned my decisions, but I was too far in to turn back. Adding to the pressure was my desire to live a morally clean life that reflected the company's objectives. Without fully understanding my business model, family, friends, and colleagues were just happy to see I was willing to put myself out there and take a risk. What they did not see was my fear and anxiety and the weight of hiding the stress I was under.

I eventually called my father for encouragement and peace of mind. It always helps to talk with him, even though I usually know what he is going to say. He always says, "You have nothing to worry about. You are special and everyone will see it. If it doesn't work out, you have lost nothing and will have gained knowledge from trying." He is always right.

I still could not escape the thoughts of failure racing through my mind. Will people support the company? Will it be financially stable? What will be the next steps once I get it started? Does it have an end game? How will I balance this with my everyday life and full-time job? Will it make the impact I want? Questions, questions, and more questions. Though stressful at the time, I believe these are normal questions when pursuing new ventures.

It was April 3, 2018, the day had finally come for me to launch Maclin Motivation LLC. Luckily, in this day and age business can conveniently reach thousands of people through social media. My plan was to launch through Facebook and LinkedIn and tag the people I wanted to notify about the business and whom I knew would share it with others. When you tag people, it allows others from their friend list to see what you are doing. I wanted as many people as possible to know about the new startup. In addition, I formatted a blanket, yet personal email to all the universities, non-profits, companies and high schools I wanted to target. The entire process was stressful, but well worth the effort and hard work.

Nervous and excited, sweating and slightly shaking, I posted the following:

> *It's finally here! Maclin Motivation! As many of you may know, I have been working on getting this started for a while. Maclin Motivation is finally here. Offering motivational enlightenment, youth and young adult transformation, leadership development, and speaking and communications consulting. Thank you for all the support. Let's make this great. Share & Follow!*
>
> *#MaclinMotivation #HustlePayThePrice*

Also, be on the lookout for Ashes & Roses, which will offer digital marketing, social media management, and website design.

Twitter: @maclin_hptp

Instagram: _maclinmotivation

Website: www.maclinmoivationhptp.com

With this announcement, I had opened a new door in my life. It was time to see if what I had been hearing all my life was true: "If you have something you want to try; just do it. You are young and have room for mistake." Fearing the responses, I would receive, or not receive, I made a commitment not to check for reactions until later in the night.

I went all day without looking on social media, checking my text messages, or monitoring my emails, but it was night and finally time to check for responses. First, I checked my phone where I had messages from friends telling me how proud they were of me and offering to share my information with different people who could use my services or help me work through the startup process. Additionally, I had over 70 text messages from family, friends, and colleagues. It was already overwhelming.

I next checked my social media accounts, Facebook and LinkedIn. Looking at Facebook, I was surprise at the support I had received. My post had 371 likes, 70 comments, and 20 shares. I was not expecting that much support at all. The comments were words of encouragement, or people tagging me to schools and programs they thought would want my services. It was an inspiring moment.

The feedback on LinkedIn was similar to that of Facebook. My colleagues, business owners, and professional network members were encouraging; with some requesting meetings to discuss how we could partner with each other or create innovative ways of outreach. In the process, I learned people have a healthy respect for people when they see they are willing to take the initiative to follow their passion. It is comparable to transitioning from being comfortable as an employee to deciding you want to hire the employees. In the space of a year, I went from employee to entrepreneur.

Finally, I checked my emails which I had used to not only let people know I had launched my business but provided information on how to book my services. I had sent 25 to 30 personal email to high school, universities, nonprofits, and corporate companies within a 2-hour radius of my home, as well as a few universities with whom I had close connections.

When I sent out these emails, I expected to receive some rejections or non-responses, but to my surprise a majority of the people I emailed responded with positive feedback. The high schools in Long Beach were so excited about my youth mentoring and outreach program that they connected me with the Long Beach Unified School District, which allowed me to become a permanent fixture in the school system. I had a speaking engagement scheduled for each week of the remaining school year. The same opportunities had afforded me with the nonprofits in Long Beach that catered to young adults. Additionally, I was tapped as the keynote speaker for several luncheons and end of the year ceremonies. The responses from the universities were very positive as well.

Everything fell into place. No, it was not easy, but persistence paid off. I had officially opened a new door in my life and all I had to do was keeping pushing forward. The more doors I pushed on, the more doors that opened. The potential for success is unlimited!

People Rich

On a summer Sunday afternoon in Long Beach I was invited to the "porch" by my good friend Marcus Tyson, a young man wise beyond his years. Marcus is a real estate investor and private company investor, who has a strong passion for philanthropy and giving back to organizations that empower youth. At the tender age of 29, he is a wealth of knowledge. The porch is the home of Wayne Chaney, Sr., a 30+ year member of the Long Beach Fire Department and an activist community leader. To truly understand how deeply he cares for the community, you have to stop by his house or more accurately, the porch.

The porch is much more than a physical place, it is a mindset; a place where men of different professions come together to just be guys and openly relax without any pressures. Men need safe spaces and places of solitude to escape from or cope with the pressures of life. I was blessed with the opportunity to experience the porch a few times. At age 26 and the youngest member of the group, I had some amazing experiences. I learned so much as I listened to these men as they enjoyed their Johnnie Walker 18 and smoked Montecristo cigars. There were decades of knowledge and life's experiences shared by those on the porch, one of whom I fondly remember was Aaron Blackburn.

"Justin," he said, "if I were here at 26, I would be a millionaire now." And, man was he right about that! Every time I left the porch, I would sit in my car and reflect on the things I had heard and think of ways to implement them in my life. So much knowledge from so many men with various interests and backgrounds. On any given Sunday, you may encounter the mayor, council members, entrepreneurs, civic leaders, lawyers, pastors, doctors, philanthropists, and people like me with aspirations to be like those men. The porch usually consisted of 10 to 15 men with different backgrounds, but all with a passion for serving others. There were usually wide-ranging conversations. One minute the conversation could be about infrastructure in Long Beach and the next minute we were talking about how to improve education for inner-city youth, followed by political issues and how they should be addressed or changed.

We always had these great conversations that could go on for hours; sometimes late into the night. Mr. Chaney always made sure to remind us that the porch was a brotherhood. His favorite slogan was, "Men, Strength and Honor!" He said it with so much conviction.

Sometimes the comment was made prior to a joking or funny comment; however, you could still feel the passion and emotion in his voice when he spoke those words. Strength and honor explained the bond between us. Wayne and the men on the porch were honest, trustworthy, responsible men of integrity and high moral character.

Though many of the men were well-established in their careers, when we talked about life and where we were at that point in time, someone frequently made the comment that it was because we had people who believed in us and supported us in our endeavors. When I think of Long Beach, I immediately think of Wayne Chaney, Sr., the work he has done for the city outside of his employment and the numerous people he has mentored from the porch.

People often ask me how I have been able to be a mover and shaker or how do I get easily involved when attacking a new venture. My reply is that even though I am not financially rich, I am rich in people. I moved from Baton Rouge, Louisiana to Long Beach California without knowing a single soul, but I choose to believe that in some small way I have made a difference. I became immersed in the city and community involvement. By volunteering my time and allowing myself to be a servant to those who needed me, I have met some amazingly smart, caring, and influential individuals; a resource much more valuable than money.

Many millennials think of money as the "be-all and end-all." I have had discussions with some of my peers who would take a job making more money, rather than make less money and fulfill their passion. There are those who have told me they only use money to help fund their passion. I have also had conversations with those who were well-off financially but gave it all up to find their purpose and live their dream. Ironically, those people are the ones who appear to be the happiest.

People, and the relationships you build with them, can be the currency that keeps on giving. When I first moved to Long Beach, CA, from Baton Rouge, LA, to work at Long Beach State, the only people I knew were those who hired me. I had recently graduated with my master's degree from LSU and the only money I had in my pocket was the $325 loan from my father. I was living in a city with an average household income of $77,000 and my beginning salary, which was less than half that amount, had to cover my $1,200 a month rent and other expenses. From those numbers you would assume I was living in poverty; yet, I never felt that way.

Trust me it was far from easy being thousands of miles away from family and friends, but then I gradually started meeting some amazing people. One of the first individuals I met was Todd Mason, a major supporter of my employer, fraternity brother, and an all-around amazing guy. We arranged to meet and hit it off immediately. He advised me that the first person I needed to meet was Mrs. Caroline Smith-Watts. Caroline is a lady of the ages, a long-time resident of Long Beach who tells it straight, but with love. I called her immediately and we set up a date to meet at her favorite Starbucks in Signal Hill. If you know Caroline, this is her favorite meeting spot. We sat down and she started the conversation, "So tell me about yourself and what do you do?" I told her my background and how I came to be in Long Beach. After presenting her with details of my life, there was no need for me to say anything else.

She told me about her upbringing in Michigan and her move to Long Beach without ever looking back. Through her many activities in Long Beach, she is seen as a community leader and the go-to person for interested in learning how they can positively impact the city. After talking with her for an hour, she figuratively gave me the blueprint for, not only making Long Beach home, but getting my career off the ground.

"The ability to serve is a powerful thing," she explained. "I gave my life to serving the people of Long Beach and making this community a better place. If you take care of Long Beach, it will take care of you. Here are some people you should reach out to for your job and for personal gain." Caroline gave me a list of contacts and I reached out to everyone on the list. At the end of our meeting, she invited me and Stephanie Baugh, Coordinator for Student-Athlete Development at Long Beach State University, to the "Country Club Gathering," her annual cook-out which brings together family, friends, and community leaders. In addition to the food and camaraderie, the event recognizes those who have made significant contributions to the city. In addition, small businesses are given the opportunity to promote their products and/or services. This country gathering is the epitome of the Long Beach I had come to know as I reached out to the contacts Caroline had given me. I experienced people who were genuine, generous, and truly wanted to make a positive difference in the city they called home.

They all invited me to meet with them at their businesses, help support their organizations, and even contribute to whatever aspiration I had in my life, whether it be with my professional career at Long Beach State University or my personal endeavors. I was overwhelmed by all they were affording me; they opened the door for me to be successful. What I immediately noticed was how no one ever talked about their money. Many people when you talk to them in other places they ask, "What is this going to do for me?", "How will this bring in revenue for us?", or "Is this worth my time? Time is money?". No one cared about anything but allowing me to make Long Beach and myself a better person. I instantly became rich in people.

It reminded me of this book called the Philosophy of Genius by Eric Weiner. In the book he goes around touring different countries to see where their Genius lies. He went to Athens to study the genius of Socrates and Aristotle, he went Hangzhou to study the genius of the Chinese culture and their slight brilliance of upgrading others creations and he went to Florence to study the genius of their art, which was based on riches and money.

Florence stood out most to me because of how they view art and money. He focused on the Medici's of Florence, which was a wealthy country, who valued innovation and art. They were the type of people who wanted the best of the best of the best, so when they had everything, they wanted they would pay people to be more innovative. This is why art was so important to them. They really appreciated the arts for what it is was, which is why Michelangelo became such a prominent figure in Florence. Michelangelo lived a very minimalist and frugal life. Eric Weiner said, "Even when he reached a certain level of riches and wealth, he still survived off a single crust of bread and glass of wine, while barely bathing and sleeping in his boots."

He was found to have enough money to buy Florence, but the concept and possession of money was meaningless to him. The only thing he lived for was his art. This reminds me of many of the people I've been blessed to encounter over the years, especially in Long Beach. Except it's not art for them, it is the people and the community. They could have all the money in the world, but it doesn't matter to them; the success and happiness of others around them is what's most important.

Many artists do not strive for being wealthy, they strive to make enough to continue supporting their passion of the arts. Monetary riches tend to cause complacency, and artist can't afford complacency; they need the struggles of life so they can be able to express at the highest level. They community leaders here in Long Beach are very much the same as artists. They have an artistry of connecting people and helping sustain a village. Many of them aren't monetarily rich but have enough to continue their artistry of bringing people together and creating a better situation for the city they love so much. In its purest form it is one of the most beautiful things you could ever see.

I had a friend and budding entrepreneur comment on how well my business was doing and the number of invitations I was receiving for speaking engagements. He wanted to know how I was able to grow the business. My response to him was that my success was due in large part to the relationships that I had developed, both personally and professionally. I told him that I believed the people I had met and the way I made them feel contributed to the growth of the business. It is not as if I had done something extraordinary, but rather I embrace people for who they are and try to use what I know how to help them reach their goals.

My friend was listening to me, but I sensed that he was frustrated with my reply. He had lived in Long Beach for over three years, knew a large number of people, but he had not created any meaningful relationships. At the time of this conversation, we were attending the book signing for Dr. Matthew Jenkins, author of *Positive Possibilities*, the author I wrote about in an earlier chapter. I asked him to look around the room.

"Do you see all these people here?" I asked. "I have a meaningful relationship with everyone here." I had helped many of the people in the room with their nonprofits, personally met with others to talk about my aspirations, and the only reason I was at the book signing was because another friend, who was in attendance, had asked me to read the book. That night he made a decision to become more disciplined and intentional in his dealing with people. He changed his mind set of using people as resources to ways he could be a resource for people. My friend had a life-changing experience that changed the trajectory of his life and you can as well; if you figure out what it means to be people rich. It is all in the philosophy of HUSTLE.

Dying Young

In 2018, within the span of one month, two of my close friends passed, one from a long-term illness, and the other from injures received in an automobile accident. Both deaths were shocking and unexpected and left me with questions without answers. Why are some people chosen before others? What is my reason for living? Will I fulfill my purpose? The realization that each breath I take may possibly be my last often awakens me in the middle of the night with cold sweats.

I have heard people say they are ready to die because they know where they will go. As a Christian, I believe the Bible has answers for all my questions, but sometimes I wish I could get into Jesus's head and just dialogue with Him about some of my concerns. Perhaps, some of my angst is a lack of fully understanding my purpose in life and whether or not I will be able to fulfill my purpose. Too often I spend time seeking answers for an endless number of questions, rather than focusing on what God has shown me to do. I believe God sometimes reveals Himself and His purpose for our lives in the death of others.

During my speaking engagements, I often talk about my cousin, Erin Hammond, who died too young from a rare disease at the age of 19.

Erin Hammond was a special girl, with whom I made many memories. Erin and my cousin, Bryce Smith, were the first people I saw grow from babies to teenagers. Though, I was only five years older than Erin, I was the big boy.

Erin was the first person with whom I had an experience that taught me the importance of responsibility and the resulting consequences of disobedience. My Aunt Ellen tells me the story all the time and I remember it vividly; every single detail. She was babysitting me while my mother ran an errand. I was 5 years old and Erin was just a little baby; crawling, but not yet able to walk or talk. One day Aunt Ellen, walked up to me and gave me this one big boy task.

"Justin, I have to step outside for a second. I need you to do something important. I need you to stay inside and watch Erin for a couple of minutes. Do not come outside, because if you do, we will all be locked outside. Can you do this?" Of course, my answer was, "Yes."

Aunt Ellen trusted me with this task to do as she had asked and went outside as she told me she unable to recall exactly what I wanted, it was probably something minor like my questions usually were: "Can I have some candy or cake?" or "Can I watch TV or play in the backyard?" Minor things a 5-year-old would think to ask. In the meantime, Erin was crawling back and forth in the den, happily minding her own business. She was a good baby!

With my question, or whatever I had on my mind that was so urgent, I opened the door and walked outside; doing exactly what my Aunt Ellen told me not to do. As soon as I did, I heard Aunt Ellen scream, "JUSTIN! What are you doing?" I had forgotten the door would lock automatically if I opened and closed it. The second I stepped outside, not only did I get a yelling from Aunt Ellen, but Erin started yelling at me as well. Her cries were loud!

After Aunt Ellen finished telling me what I had done wrong, she pointed me towards the door and told me to sing to Erin to help her stop crying. All I could think of was Barney's, my favorite purple dinosaur, theme song; I *Love You*. When I think about it now, Barney was pretty creepy, but at this moment he was my saving grace. I began singing the song:

"I love you, you love me,

We're a happy family,

With a great big hug,

And a kiss from me to you,

Won't you say you love me too?

I love you, you love me,

We're the best!"

I will never forget staring at Erin and singing to her through the storm door. The moment I started singing, she immediately stopped crying. While Aunt Ellen and I waited outside for someone to bring us a key to get back inside the house, I sang this song repeatedly for about 30 minutes or longer. Whenever I would stop singing, Aunt Ellen, would shout, "Sing Justin." If I knew then what I know now, I would have taken her response to my singing as a sign of my great vocals and my ability to serenade people with my voice. Can you imagine what a good singer you have to be to get a small baby to stop crying? Well, let me tell you; you have to be one heck of a vocalist, and I was.

Finally, someone arrived to unlock the door and we went inside where Erin was sitting and content. We knew she was safe because we could see her through the storm door while I was keeping her engaged. This was my first memory of being given a responsibility, and it started with Erin. Throughout the years, we grew closer and shared many good memories. In so many ways, she was wise beyond her years. When I first started taking basketball seriously, it was Erin who taught me how to do a left-handed layup.

Uncle Marvin, Erin's dad, was one of the first people to encourage me to play basketball. He is a basketball fanatic who was a better-than-average high school player. His backyard coaching was a major factor in helping, Marcus, my older cousin, successfully compete in high school and become a scholarship basketball player at The College of Charleston in Charleston, SC. For years he begged and pleaded with my mother to allow me to play basketball. She did not relent until he introduced her to Clyde Peete, my first formal basketball coach.

When I first joined the team, I literally did not know anything about the game, nor could I do anything on the court. Sure, I knew the ball was round and went through a net, but beyond that I was clueless. I was reminiscent of the old adage, "You can't chew gum and walk at the same time." To help me with my development we visited Uncle Marvin, as we usually did every Sunday, but now we would go to the backyard to work on my basketball skills. The main areas of my workouts would primarily focus on my mid-range jump shot, ball handling drills, free throws and the dreaded left-handed layup.

Practice always went well until I got to the left-handed layup. My footwork was off balance, my left hand seemed too weak to make the shot, (my right hand is dominant) and overall, I was just not very coordinated. I probably missed 10 to 15 shots in a row, and if the attempts looked as bad as they felt I could see why my Uncle had gotten a little frustrated. He looked at me and said, "Stop!" He then called Erin over and asked her to do a left-handed layup. Erin walked over, took the ball away from me, and gave me a look as to say, "Watch and learn!" She completed the left-handed layup with ease. Left foot, right foot, jumps up with the ball in her left hand, the ball hits the top left corner of the backboard box, and goes in without touching the rim. My uncle went inside the house, leaving me with my new coach.

Erin literally stayed outside with me and walked me through the process of making a left-handed layup until I finally made a couple in a row. With each shot, I felt my confidence grow. This was a major accomplishment for me at this stage of my young life. I wanted and needed to become better if I were to get playing time on the team. Erin's coaching took me from a player who had a lot of bench time to a more consistent player who received more playing time. What I learned from her on that Sunday afternoon was a skill that I needed when my high school basketball team won the state championship. It all worked together for my good.

Erin was a confident young lady and excelled at everything she attempted. In elementary school, she was the go-to player on the basketball team. During the summer, she played soccer and softball. When she was-nine-years old, Erin was introduced to karate, which became her life-long passion. She became a fourth-degree black belt who competed in and won many local and national competitions. Her influence continues till this day with the children she taught in karate classes. When she passed, I thought about the impact she had on me and our entire family. I wonder if she knew that helping me learn how to make a layup would be a critical factor in my overall development? From our Aunt Peaches, the family matriarch, to Bryce, our youngest cousin, she amazed and inspired us all. I want to embody the kind of spirit she possessed, that of wanting the best for herself and for others. Erin left our family a legacy that will never be forgotten. She fulfilled her life's purpose!

Winning Is Not Everything

Win! Win at all costs! How important is winning, does it really matter, or does it sometime matter and at other times not? Often when one wins, another has to lose. I have had contact with many individuals who have a lot to offer but lack the discipline and competitiveness to make a significant difference. Comments, or excuses, I have heard include: "I'm just not a competitive type of person," or "It just doesn't matter that much to me." Or the old standby, "If it's meant to be, it's meant to be." Because I consider myself a disciplined person, it is extremely difficult for me to relate to that philosophy.

When I talk to students about exercising discipline in their lives in order to reach a goal, they want to know how I am able to follow through and stay the course. My answer is two-fold; I like a good challenge, and I like to win. My road to becoming a vegetarian started with a bet that I could not go meatless for a week. I won the bet, discovered that I actually like it and now live a vegetarian lifestyle. This same principle applied to my football career, which ultimately afforded me the opportunity to be offered athletic scholarships at several powerhouse football schools before accepting a scholarship to LSU.

It is this same desire to win and be successful that brought me from Memphis, Tennessee to California. I was told the transition would be difficult and I would not make it on the West Coast, but I was determined to prove that I could. Though my parents were divorced, they were both an intricate part of my life and deserve credit for instilling in me a strong work ethic and sense of self-worth, combined with a you can "do it" attitude. A winning philosophy dares one to seek out and take advantage of opportunities. Today, Maclin Motivation exists not because of fear of failure, but because I chose to not let others' pessimism deter me from what I consider my calling. Of course, there were the skeptics with their questions and concerns. "What do you have to share that can help people? You haven't been through enough. You are too young to be transformative." But the winner in me was determined to start a program with the express purpose of youth empowerment using the HUSTLE philosophy.

In some sectors, individual wins have been replaced with the theory that all participants, regardless of the amount of personal input, receive a prize. How does this hamper individual pursuit of success? I am reminded of former New England Patriots and Pittsburg Steelers player, James Harrison, who was an undrafted free agent who became an

NFL Super Bowl Champion. He often spoke of how he felt others took his love and heart for the game of football for granted because he was shorter than most, lacked technical skills, and was not as athletic as others who played his position. Those were things he could not control, but he always said the one thing he could control was to be the hardest working player on the field by always being mentally and physically prepared. He played his last game at the age of 40. Who does that? Simply put, "A winner".

On a personal note, in 2015 Harrison gained some notoriety when he stripped his sons of "non-winning" participation trophies. According to Harrison, "Everything in life should be earned. . . cause sometimes your best is not enough, and that should drive you to want to do better...not cry and whine until somebody gives you something to shut u up and keep you happy." Participating is part of the process but only a small percentage of the outcome when you think about all it takes to win.

One of my first realizations of the pain of losing occurred when I was a third-grader in a small Christian school called Christ the Rock in Memphis, Tennessee. My mother was very persistent about me getting a better education than the other African American children I grew up around and keeping me away from ending up in situations I could potentially fail in. This caused her to make the decision to attempt to let me go to a private school and see how it went. Before going to this school, I went to Ross Elementary in East Memphis which was a primarily African American school. Christ the Rock was the completely opposite as you could imagine. It was a predominantly white school but had a very welcoming atmosphere but that didn't stop me from feeling like an outcast in many ways. I can only recall there being maybe a couple other children who looked like me, plus academically I could see the disparity on a daily bases. After this one-year stint at the small private school of Christ the Rock it showed to not be the place for me and I ended up going back to Ross Elementary.

As I recall, the primary curriculum focused on Bible class and spelling & grammar. The highlight of the year was the annual Spelling Bee Contest. Whomever won the contest received a large trophy and other prizes. I just knew I was going to win this spelling bee at all costs; even though at that time I did not know what at all cost meant.

The spelling bee was on a Friday morning and would continue throughout the entire school day. I did study some words in preparation for the contest, but inevitably, I talked myself into thinking I was smart enough to need only minimal preparation for the event. In my mind, I was a winner and had automatic favor over my life. I would get the perfect draw of words that I knew how to spell. This approach backfired on me in the most embarrassing way imaginable for a 3rd grader who thought he knew it all. The competition was held in the auditorium in front of the entire 3rd grade where students would be called onto the stage in alphabetical order by last name. My last name was Maclin, which put me in the middle of the group of students. My chances were good and would play to my advantage; I was not too close to the front or too close to the end of students.

There were approximately 20 to 30 children in front of me; all of whom were given words I could spell with ease. Finally, it was my turn and I walk confidently to the stage and was given the word "grapefruit." I spelled it with no problem. I made it past the first round and knew I have the competition in the bag. Little did I know those fruits would come back to bite me in the end. We begin the 2nd round of the competition and at this point four people misspelled their word and were eliminated from the competition. I remember it so vividly because one of the people I thought I was smarter than got one of the easiest words wrong. I thought: Like how? What was he thinking? Get it together!

As we began the second round, the people ahead of me also started to misspell words, which oddly built my confidence. It is weird how sometimes seeing others fail, gives you a sense of confidence. It is simply an opportunity to solidify your goal and see those people who are obstacles moved out the way. In this spelling bee, I ended being one of those obstacles that ended up getting out of somebody's way. My turn had arrived, and I walked on the stage with my head held high; then the announcer gave me my word. The word was "B-A-N-A-N-A," and I confidently spelled it "B-A-N-N-A-N-A." I looked up as if I knew it was correct. Of course, I was informed it was wrong and told I was eliminated from the competition.

This was the first time that it really mattered to me that I had been defeated and was a loser. Of course, I had had losses, but never on the big stage in front of a crowd where the outcome was solely on me. At this point, the only times I experienced major losses were in a team environment where I never felt I was the sole reason for the loss. The spelling bee was all on me. I lost because of my lack of preparation, my lack of intensity, and my lack of humility.

Though a small incident when compared to other experiences I have had in my life, I learned the value of planning and preparation to be successful in life. Having unlimited success in life-changing experience is all it's about. The only way you can have success after these life-changing experiences is if you internalize the situations that happen to you each time. This is why 18 years later, I can recall the 3rd grade spelling bee contest. For years I have replayed that loss in my mind, forcing me to face the reason for my dismal failure all those years ago.

This is the process I use when traumatic events occur in my life. It is as if I am a mad scientist analyzing the how, what, when, and where in order to avoid a repeat occurrence. Now, I am at a point in my life where the desire to win is a part of who I am, and I have developed coping mechanisms when I do not win. I have had good outcomes and some not so good, but I have learned to stay in the game. The philosophy of HUSTLE is about perseverance and the will to win. Reflect on your happenings and use them to better yourself. Use them to be the person you want to be even though when they happened you weren't anywhere close to where you should have been. Let's us hustle and pay the price daily for what we deserve and what our family deserve. Winning isn't everything, it's the only thing. Allow your hustle and the feeling of life victory to be your foundation.

Acknowledgements

Hustle Pay the Price: The Philosophy of HUSTLE is a short, self-help book focusing on events that have shaped my personal and career development. This opportunity would not have been possible without the love, support, guidance, and wisdom of the many people who have unconditionally encouraged and supported me. I love you all deeply.

Family: Lisa Love, James Maclin, Pechone Love, Karol Maclin, Everlina Hull, Arthur Hull, Josephine Hammond, Marvin Hammond, Ellen Hammond, Sarah Maclin, Erin Hammond, Marcus Hammond, Vickie Smith, Bryce Smith, Krystal Maclin, Katika Davis, Kristian Myers, Kwinci Britt, Sarah Maclin, Uncle Jerry, the whole family from Covington, Tennessee

Friends: Ferious Williams, Desi T & Desi J, Joe Hollins, Josh Hollins, Dexter Alexander, Jeremy Peeples, J.C. Copeland, Jodi Calloway, Brian Johnson, Lubbock Smith, Tarik Black, Maurice Savage, Eric Whalum, Tim Peete, Tre' Sullivan, Jarrett Hardnett, Marquel Pope, Jordyn Warren

Louisiana State University Master's Family: BB Bynum, Shaquille Lowe, Sakiya Gallon. Erika Holland, Shanekia Hall, Llomincia Hall, Dr. Jennifer Curry, Dr. Roland Mitchell, Michael Coleman, Wilton Jackson

Long Beach, CA Family: Marcus Tyson, Wayne Chaney, Sr., Walter Larkins, Aaron Blackburn, Wayne Stickney, Todd Mason, Kristen Lease, Carolyn Smith-Watts, Lesia Anderson, Long Beach School District, The Long Beach Rotary Club, Lakewood Toastmasters Club

Key Influencers: Louisiana State University Staff and Faculty; Long Beach State University Staff and Faculty; University of Davis California Staff and Faculty; Tim Duncan; Derek Horne; Kappa Alpha Psi Fraternity Incorporated; Pastor Johnny and Shelly Hollins, Jubilee Christian Center, Baton Rouge, LA; Pastor Bill Adkins, Greater Imani Church, Memphis, TN; Coach Clyde Peete; Eric Watson Sr., The Ridgeway High School Family

There are many others who have had a major impact on my life. You know who you are, and I thank you all.